Language and Language Learning

LINGUISTICS AND STYLE

Language and Language Learning

Edited by RONALD MACKIN and PETER STREVENS

Linguistics and Style

On defining style:
an essay in applied linguistics

NILS ERIK ENKVIST

An approach
to the study of style

JOHN SPENCER
MICHAEL GREGORY

Volume edited by John Spencer

LONDON
Oxford University Press

Oxford University Press, Ely House, London W.1

GLASGOW NEW YORK TORONTO MELBOURNE WELLINGTON
CAPE TOWN SALISBURY IBADAN NAIROBI DAR ES SALAAM LUSAKA ADDIS ABABA
BOMBAY CALCUTTA MADRAS KARACHI LAHORE DACCA
KUALA LUMPUR SINGAPORE HONG KONG TOKYO

ISBN 0 19 437016 X

© *Oxford University Press, 1964*

First published 1964
Reprinted 1965, 1967, *and* 1971

PRINTED IN GREAT BRITAIN BY
HAZELL WATSON AND VINEY LTD
AYLESBURY, BUCKS

Contents

Introduction

FEW literary scholars would suggest that literature can be satisfactorily studied without due attention to its medium, language. Nor would many linguists justify the investigation of literary language without guidance from those who devote themselves to the study of literature. There would, moreover, be a measure of agreement on both sides that the student of literature, whatever his particular interests, ought to be trained in the study of both language and literature. Yet, beneath this appearance of politeness and mutual esteem, discord and tension sometimes manifest themselves between what have become distinct disciplines.

It would be possible to argue that until recently no real dichotomy between linguistic and literary studies existed, and that scholars in both branches traditionally collaborated in an atmosphere of accord, to the extent that their interests and problems overlapped. In the field of English studies, with which we are concerned, this mutuality of interest seems to be confirmed by the work of many great scholars, such as R. W. Chambers or C. S. Lewis, who were at home in both philology and literary studies, and in whose work the one supports and nourishes the other. This prelapsarian picture of English studies in the past would suggest that it was the development of modern descriptive linguistics into an autonomous discipline—a discipline perhaps often less grateful to its parent philology than a thriving son should be—which induced the tensions inescapable, so romantic writers tell us, in any triangular relationship, especially one in which rejection of the father may imply Freudian complications.

It is true that modern linguistics achieved what autonomy it possesses by turning its back, at least for a time, upon the historical and comparative preoccupations of traditional philology, focussing much of its attention on the task of describing exotic languages, many of them with no written history. It thus concentrated upon the structure, rather than the history, of languages, and to do so began to construct heuristic models for the purpose of describing language structure. In its task of description linguistics was greatly aided by its sister discipline, phonetics, which, over the decades, made available a wider and more sophisticated understanding of the nature and function of speech. Traditional theories of language, and accepted methods and emphases in language study, increasingly, and at times brashly, came under question. The link between literary studies and the new linguistics became exceedingly tenuous, as many linguists came to feel that they had more in common with the anthropologist or the social scientist than with the historian or the aesthetician. And although the relationship between philology and linguistics was never broken, these two branches of language study also diverged, as their interests and methods became, at least in some areas, markedly and necessarily different.

In the meantime, however, English literary studies had also, in some quarters, made a bid for autonomy. Growing specialization, and the consequent compartmentalization of all branches of academic study, undoubtedly contributed to this. But other influences were also at work. The decline in dominance of classical studies during the previous decades offered English literary studies the opportunity to put itself forward as the alternative, as a new basis for the type of education so long associated with the classics. In presenting their discipline as a source of moral and social insights, as a new core subject for humanistic education, F. R. Leavis and his associates of the thirties led the way. Their influence upon the remodelling of syllabuses in departments of English has probably been as great, in the long run, as their impact upon literary criticism. Thus, in many parts of the world today, it is possible for students to follow courses in English literature without any necessary requirement to study the language and its history. For, in making this claim for the central place of English studies in a humanistic education, F. R. Leavis felt that the discipline should be emancipated from its old association with 'linguistic and philology'.

Today, as a result of the demands of communication engineering, machine translation and the ever-growing need for efficient English language teaching all over the world, linguists have become involved as never before in the study of contemporary English. They come to this task armed with fresh insights and new theories, as well as a formidable technical vocabulary. Their work in certain areas of this field of investigation has brought about a renewed confrontation of linguistic and literary studies, a confrontation not unattended at times with mutual suspicion. Here, within a microcosm of the wider division between the sciences and the humanities, failures of communication on both sides sometimes darken the relationship. In this situation it would be idle to blame literary studies for a kind of out-of-date feudalism, or linguistics for an assertive neocolonialism, or historical philology for an effete neutralism, for none of these caps fits very well; and indeed, it is only at certain points of overlap that there is likelihood of conflict or misunderstanding. Nevertheless, as the academic world is becoming increasingly aware, it is often within the overlapping areas of two or more distinct but related disciplines that the growing points of creative research and teaching lie. And it is through collaboration in joint enterprises in such areas that disciplines which have grown apart can begin afresh to appreciate the particular insights and methods which each has developed out of its own specialized preoccupations.

One of these areas of overlap is the study of style. Here literary and linguistic studies meet; and the modern descriptive linguist must, in this field, seek also the assistance of the historian of the language. The linguist who dismisses the sensitive intuitive response of a literary scholar as being inaccessible to objective verification, or who disregards the work of the traditional philologist as lacking in rigour, or, on the other hand, the literary scholar who rejects as inelegant, and irrelevant to any aspects of the study of literature, the linguist's painstaking attempts to arrive at a measure of objectivity and explicitness in his description of the complex structure of language—neither of these is likely to contribute to the development of stylistic studies.

Fortunately, however, such thorough-going academic chauvinism is rare. For one thing, not all centres of English studies broke with the earlier tradition of maintaining and strengthening the ties between the study of literature and the study of language. Nor have all such centres been inhospitable to new developments in linguistics. And by no means all modern linguists, especially those whose major focus of interest has been the study of the English language, severed their connexions with literary studies or historical philology; many of them, indeed, were trained in these related disciplines before they became acquainted with the theories and methods of descriptive linguistics. To the latter category belong the three contributors to this volume. As they emphasize, familiarity with all three branches of study is a necessary prerequisite for anyone who wishes to undertake work in the field of style.

That style is a highly complex phenomenon, which can be viewed from many different points of view, is exemplified in Nils Erik Enkvist's monograph, in which he examines the diversity of definitions which have been found for it. His purpose in pursuing the manifold definitions of style is to find the common elements, as a prolegomenon to his consideration of a problem of great relevance to the advanced teaching of English overseas. Universities in which English is an important foreign or second language are increasingly aware that neither the old prescription for a syllabus in English, that it should consist of a judicious mixture of historical philology and literature, nor the new, that it should consist of literature alone, is fully satisfactory. In neither case is the student given any systematic training in relating differences in the use of language to the social, technical, rhetorical, or aesthetic functions which these serve. Such a student, if he has had a sound linguistic training, may be able to describe in considerable detail the linguistic differences he observes in a variety of English texts, spoken and written; but, having little acquaintance with English-speaking societies, he has only a very limited empirical knowledge of the restrictions which are placed upon the ranges of language deemed appropriate to different circumstances and different functions. He is thus in some respects in the position of a man able to describe in minute detail the shape and composition of the carpenter's various tools, yet ignorant of the functions for which the craftsman uses them. Such inability to relate *stylo-linguistics* to *stylo-behaviouristics*, as Enkvist calls these two aspects of stylistics, can be a severe handicap, not only in developing skill in and responsiveness to the language, but in the study of literature too. For, as both monographs in this volume suggest, the study of style is wider than the study of literature. To view style in literature against the background of the whole range of norms which a language develops in subserving the needs of the society which uses it, is to add a perspective to stylistic study from which the examination of language in literature cannot fail to benefit.

It may be thought that the English-speaking student, brought up from childhood in an English language environment, will have no difficulties in this respect. Certainly he will have learnt empirically a great deal about linguistic appropriateness in many different social and functional situations. He is rarely, however, able to analyse and classify these differences; nor will his range of experience be in any sense complete. It may not, for one thing, have an articulated historical dimension. Thus the development and application of *institutional* categories, synchronically and diachronically, may be seen as one of the tasks awaiting the student of style.

A writer's style may be regarded as an individual and creative utilization of the resources of language which his period, his chosen dialect, his genre and his purpose within it offer him. To understand and to make explicit his linguistic creativity, to appreciate in full the alchemy by which he transmutes the base metal of everyday language into the gold of art, it is first necessary to recognize and where possible to specify the ranges of language within which he is working and upon which he is able to draw. To attempt to do so in analytical detail is not to destroy the wonder of literature; rather it should enhance it. The second monograph in this volume attempts briefly to suggest one approach towards this end.

Throughout both monographs references are made to modern descriptive linguistics, especially where its methods and procedures seem relevant to the study of style. In many instances areas of research are indicated, and it will be clear to any careful reader that the descriptive study of language both within English literature and outside it is still very incomplete. Those who come to the subject without much knowledge of modern linguistics, but who are stimulated to explore further, either for the purpose of developing new courses or out of personal interest, may find the brief bibliography appended to this volume helpful. Those who are conversant with linguistics but who do not have much knowledge of the contribution of literary scholars to the study of style may care to examine some of the works included in the first section of the bibliography.

It is hoped that this small volume may contribute to the current rethinking of the relationship between linguistic and literary studies, and offer a stimulus, and perhaps some assistance, to the many teachers of English in schools and universities in Britain and overseas who would like to make this relationship a reality in their teaching and research.

Leeds.   John Spencer.

May 1964.

On defining style

AN ESSAY IN APPLIED LINGUISTICS

NILS ERIK ENKVIST

1

LIKE children at the feet of a conjurer, people react to style with varying attitudes. Some simply relax and enjoy the effects, and perhaps later recollect their emotions in tranquillity. Others feel the naughty boy's urge to peep up the performer's sleeve and to expose the partitions of his hat, even at the risk of ignoring part of the show and of irritating the rest of the audience. I must say at once that in this essay my purpose and approach have little to do with the enjoyment and elegant description of literary qualities. I shall merely try to define, as tersely as I can, what I have come to regard as the most essential traits that set style apart from other levels of language. Nor have I had any chance of forgetting that many of my sentences and paragraphs could be expanded into bulky volumes without exhausting their subject. All my theorizing will be slanted towards an answer to one single, practical question: What must we do to give students of a foreign language a sense of style in that language?

It is symptomatic of our age, and most regrettable, that literary scholars and professional linguists often find themselves on different sides of a mountain-like barrier, with philologists struggling for a precarious foothold on one slope or the other. To re-establish contact across the top, neither loud shouting nor the use of philologists as errand-boys is enough. What we need is a well-designed tunnel dug from both ends. Fortunately the problems of style no longer seem hopelessly buried under the Alps that separate the study of literature from modern linguistics. Thanks not least to methods of close reading and new criticism, many literary scholars have given up their former preoccupation with background studies. They have worked down to detailed analysis of selected textual features and of the responses such features provoke in the reader. Meanwhile linguists too are beginning to mine the same territory from claims they have staked at their side of the barrier. Most of them are inching their way towards style from the study of smaller linguistic units and patterns.

Yet it would be sanguine to expect the tunnels of the linguists and the literary critics automatically to meet in the middle of the mountain. To the former, the investigation of style is essentially a scientific description of certain types and sets of linguistic structures that occur in a given text, and of their distribution. On the contrary, the literary scholar must be more preoccupied with matters outside the text. Thus he will study the reader's responses and his linking of given textual stimuli with features that lie beyond the text itself but are part of his past experience recalled by stimuli in the text. Only the literary scholar can tell us all that is implied in Milton's making Comus the son of Circe by Bacchus. The full implications of Comus' sinister ancestry do not emerge from a linguistic description of Milton's text, nor even from a linguistic analysis of the whole corpus of English literature. Yet they must be understood for a proper appreciation of Milton's poem.

In advanced foreign-language teaching we are, and should be, much preoccupied with literature. It is nowadays taken for granted that university students read a large amount of poetry and prose in the foreign languages they choose for a degree. With rising standards in the schools, secondary-school teachers of languages are also increasingly concerned with literary texts. Many of them feel obliged to give their pupils more than the traditional grammatical and lexical commentaries on the poems, short stories, plays, and novels that are read intensively in the classroom and extensively outside it. At least in Scandinavia, some teachers claim to be ill-equipped for this task. Even those who were trained in first-language subjects in which literary analysis plays a prominent part have frequently hesitated before adapting and applying their literary methods to a fundamentally different teaching situation. At the same time we still seem to be short of background theory and of methods designed for the teaching of literature in a foreign language. Between grammar and literary history there lies a no-man's land mapped neither by traditional foreign-language textbooks nor by school or university texts designed for first-language students. This is one of the areas in which a definition and theory of style might be of use.

The study of all texts, including literary ones, has several functions in foreign-language teaching. One of them is to provide a short-cut to the extensive experience of linguistic items in context that native speakers acquire by direct exposure. Ideally, the student ought to learn to respond to textual stimuli in the manner of a suitably selected informant. Such responses may be regarded as part of the total meaning of the text in question. As in the choice of dialect, norm, register, and pronunciation, the selection of a suitable model response must in practice be based on sociolinguistic and institutional considerations. The students' abilities and the limitations of the teaching facilities must of course also be thought of. This is neither more nor less than what happens in all teaching of literature and indeed in all education, one of whose basic aims is the transmission of cultural heritage in terms of approved behaviour patterns.

What, then, must the student know, and what must he be able to do, before he can respond to textual stimuli in the approved manner? I suppose all the aims and goals of foreign-language teaching could be marched forth as part of the answer. One feature I wish to emphasize here is that he has to know the language well enough to distinguish between common and rare types of linguistic behaviour in a given context and situation. *Realia* are necessary too, and they become even more important if the two cultures reflected in the source and target languages differ owing to great distances in space or time, or to great contrasts in cultural traditions. Like the native, the foreign-language

5

student must also learn to react to literary features of the text including its literary structure and philosophy.

One major problem, therefore, in the teaching of a foreign language is giving the student a sense of style. This problem cannot be side-stepped in any reading of texts, and least of all in the advanced study of literary ones. To give a pupil a feeling for style we should not only provide him with linguistic descriptions of the text in terms of one or another set of linguistic categories. We must also teach him to react to textual stimuli in the approved manner. It would simplify this task if we could agree on the nature of stylistic stimuli, or, in other words, define what style is. If we can accurately pin-point those textual features that cause stylistic responses in our chosen native informant, we may hope to add yet another weapon to our arsenal of teaching methods.

2

LET us first very briefly recall a few of the classic approaches to style. A full survey would be complicated by the fact that, through the ages, linguistics and literary analysis have met, or clashed, on the territory of style.[1] Indeed to trace the borderline between linguistics and literary analysis through history involves rewriting the annals of both disciplines from a special, and very rewarding,

1. Here, as elsewhere in this essay, I must refrain from citing anything like a full, or even select, bibliography, whose compilation would be a major research project in its own right. Together with standard linguistic and literary bibliographies, the notes given below and the final bibliography in this volume will provide the reader with materials for further study.

A very concise attempt at setting various views of style into their historical and philosophical context is available in Pierre Guiraud, *La stylistique*, Que sais-je?, Paris, 1961.

point of view. So mediaeval *grammatica* included the study of literature until the triumph of logic in the twelfth and thirteenth centuries drove out *belles lettres* from the university syllabus. In the Renaissance, linguistics was usually philological in character, aiming at the editing, analysis and explication of texts without fighting shy of stylistic questions. Nineteenth and twentieth century historical and comparative linguists have often, systematically and properly, sought the support of philology, including literary aspects of textual study. A mastery of the principles at least of diachronic linguistics has been the first step in the traditional syllabus of all philologists. But few, if any, of these linguistic theories have expressly catered for the linguistics of style.

From the literary side, some aesthetic theories have made heavy inroads on traditionally linguistic territory, and also attempted to set up principles directly relevant to our present concern. Most notably, Benedetto Croce labelled the eighteenth chapter of his aesthetics as 'Identity of linguistics and aesthetics'. His whole theory amounts to an eloquent plea for the unity of aesthetics and linguistics. Expression is the focal point of Croce's thought. Language, he says, is expression, and the study of expression is the task of aesthetics; therefore both aesthetics and linguistics are concerned with one and the same phenomenon. Croce regarded language as a creative activity of the individual rather than as a system of signals shared by a group. To him, the kind of inventory of linguistic items that forms the basis of modern structuralism was too artificial to be of much value. Croce's cavalier attitude to linguistic units appears for instance in his discussion of syllabic limits:

Del resto, i limiti delle sillabe, come quelli delle parole, sono affatto arbitrari, e distinti alla peggio per uso empirico. Il parlare primitivo o il parlare dell'uomo incolto è un continuo, scompagnato da ogni coscienza di divisione del discorso in parole e sillabe, enti immaginarî foggiati dalle scuole. Su questi enti non si fonda nessuna legge di vera Linguistica. Si veda a riprova la confessione dei linguisti, che del iato, della cacofonia, della dieresi, della sineresi,

7

non vi sono veramente leggi fonetiche, ma leggi soltanto di gusto e di convenienza; il che vuol dire leggi estetiche. E quali sono poi le leggi circa le parole, che non siano insieme leggi di stile?[1]

Most of today's linguists would agree that Croce erred in postulating that the segmentation of language was arbitrary and extralinguistic. Still, the final question was well put.

The powerful influence of the Crocean aesthetic is obvious in the writings of the Italian neolinguists. Related ideas also abound in works by the Vosslerian school of idealists, whose principles culminated in the writings of Leo Spitzer. Undoubtedly the neolinguists and idealists have done valuable work in exploding some of the oversimplifications of the neogrammarians and in reminding us once again that languages are spoken and written by men and women deeply influenced by their cultural environments. Similar criticisms of the atomism of extreme neogrammarian methods have in fact reappeared in more rigorous form in some recent structural theories of language. But both neolinguistics and Vosslerian idealism fail to give us a unified theory of style and method of stylistic analysis in terms of rigorous linguistic concepts. They often emphasize subtle psychological and cultural phenomena whose study tends centrifugally to escape from the text itself. The scholar's intuitions are also given very free play. Spitzer's approach can be illustrated with a quotation:

Why do I insist that it is impossible to offer the reader a step-by-step rationale to be applied to a work of art? For one reason, that the first step on which all

---

1. *Estetica come scienza dell'espressione e linguistica generale*, Bari, 1928, p. 163. [For the rest, syllable boundaries, like those of words, are completely arbitrary, and distinguished somehow or other by empirical use. Primitive speech or the speech of uncivilized man is a continuum, unaccompanied by any awareness of the division of the utterance into words and syllables, which are imaginary units created by the schools. No true law of Linguistic is founded on these units. To prove this, one should consider how linguists admit that the laws of hiatus, cacophony, diaeresis and synaeresis are not truly phonetic, but merely laws of taste and of convenience, that is to say aesthetic laws. And what, then, are the laws about speech that are not at the same time laws of style?—*My translation. N.E.E.*]

may hinge, can never be planned: it must already have taken place. This first step is the awareness of having been struck by a detail, followed by a conviction that this detail is connected basically with the work of art; it means that one has made an 'observation',—which is the starting point of a theory, that one has been prompted to raise a question—which must find an answer . . . 'Method' is for me much more a 'habitual procedure of the mind' . . . than a 'program regulating beforehand a series of operations . . . in view of reaching a well-defined result'.[1]

In itself, Spitzer's first step—noting his own response to a literary text and studying the stimuli that provoked it—is by no means unscientific. But as long as it is unchecked by a rigorous and exhaustive linguistic analysis, the procedure may remain fragmentary and runs the risk of losing its balance and proportion through excessive introspection. At best, Spitzer and his colleagues are splendidly provocative and capable of flashes of brilliant literary insight. Yet their intuitive mentalism and wide 'humanism' is hard to combine with the systematic observation and definition of variance and invariance that underlie both neogrammarian and structural linguistics. They have not arrived at anything like a complete linguistic rationale of style.

Even if the works of literary critics of these, and countless other, schools have failed to produce a basis for a linguistic theory of style, it would be a mistake for the linguist to turn up his nose at them. On the contrary, when struggling towards the fusion of rigorous textual description with the study of representative responses to textual stimuli, we should try to profit from all the available material that contains observations restatable in linguistic terms. This enormous material includes works on style in general and studies of the style of individual writers and texts, written by literary scholars and philologists as well as by some linguists who have used a modern descriptive apparatus.

1. *Linguistics and Literary History*, Princeton, 1948, pp. 26–27 and p. 38 n. 17.

9

3

NEXT I shall glance at some of the ways in which style has been defined. 'A discussion of the word Style,' said John Middleton Murry, 'if it were pursued with only a fraction of the rigour of a scientific investigation, would inevitably cover the whole of literary aesthetics and the theory of criticism. Six books would not suffice for the attempt: much less would six lectures.'[1] All the same, an analysis of some four or five score definitions of style culled from critical works, linguistic studies, dictionaries, and encyclopedias of different periods shows that such definitions can, allowing for much overlapping, be classified under a limited number of major headings.[2]

One way to classify definitions of style is by the basic stages of the communication process. First there are definitions based on the point of view of the writer,[3] such as Goethe's in *Einfache Nachahmung der Natur, Manier, Stil*.[4] Here Goethe regards style as a higher, active principle of composition by which the writer pene-

1. *The Problem of Style*, Oxford Paperbacks, 1960, p. 3.

2. It is necessary to point out that these definitions are here quoted in their barest form, without all the conceptual frames, qualifications, and explanations with which they may be surrounded in their complete, original context. I am of course not criticizing individual works but commenting on different major approaches to style. In addition to the works quoted in the notes, helpful sources include William T. Brewster, *Representative Essays on the Theory of Style*, New York, 1913, and the introductory section of Pierre Naert, *Stilen i Vilhelm Ekelunds aforismer och essäer*, Malmö, 1949.

3. As the main concern of the present chapter is with written texts, I shall use the simple 'writer' and 'reader' even where the observations are equally valid for spoken language.

4. Discussed and quoted by Emil Ermatinger in *Das dichterische Kunstwerk*, Leipzig and Berlin, 1921, p. 199.

trates and reveals the inner form of his subject. Style is opposed to a passive imitation of nature or to the facile application of mannerisms to the subject. Secondly, there are definitions that deal with characteristics of the text itself, attempting analysis of style entirely in terms of objective investigation of textual features. Thirdly, there are definitions based on the impressions of the reader. They are extremely common in most works of literary criticism and literary history that characterize individual or group styles. Often a definition is composed of more than one of these three kinds of *dicta*. Examples of all three kinds will appear in the following.

Another distinction can be made between statements on style that are objectively verifiable and those that are subjectively impressionistic. Presumably a foreign-language teacher is best served by a definition of style making possible stylistic analyses that are operationally concrete. They should be based on those linguistic features that each student, at his particular level of progress, can verify on his own. This requirement immediately disqualifies a host of definitions, including those which merely identify style with existence or thought[1] and those which state that style involves saying the right thing in the most effective way.[2] Of the

1. e.g., 'Le style est pour nous une disposition de l'existence, une manière d'être.' (Henri Morier, *La Psychologie des styles*, Genève, 1959, p. 7) [To us, style is a disposition of existence, a way of being.] 'Style, indeed, is not really a mere invisible transparent medium, it is not really a garment but, as Gourmont said, the very thought itself. It is the miraculous transubstantiation of a spiritual body, given to us in the only form in which we may receive and absorb that body . . .' (Havelock Ellis in 'The Art of Writing', *The Dance of Life*, London, 1923, p. 163.)

2. e.g. Kenneth Burke in *Permanence and Change*, Los Altos, Calif., 1954, p. 50: 'In its simplest manifestation, style is ingratiation. It is an attempt to gain favor by the hypnotic or suggestive process of "saying the right thing".' And Sir Arthur Quiller-Couch, *On the Art of Writing*, Cambridge, 1920, p. 248: 'This then is Style. As technically manifested in Literature it is the power to touch with ease, grace, precision, any note in the gamut of human thought and emotion. But essentially it resembles good manners.'

remaining approaches, six will be mentioned in the following: style as a shell surrounding a pre-existing core of thought or expression; as the choice between alternative expressions; as a set of individual characteristics; as deviations from a norm; as a set of collective characteristics; and as those relations among linguistic entities that are statable in terms of wider spans of text than the sentence.

First, then, some examples of definitions that regard style as an addition to a central core of thought or expression:

Style consists in adding to a given thought all the circumstances calculated to produce the whole effect that the thought ought to produce.[1]

Here Stendhal apparently took for granted the existence of the 'given thought' *per se* before its final verbalization. To him, style was an addition whose function was defined not in terms of beauty but more inclusively in terms of expediency and effect.

Once style is regarded as an addition, it becomes possible to conceive of utterances that have no style. In *Counter-Statement*, Kenneth Burke thus regards manner and style as characteristic only of eloquent works, not of uneloquent ones, though presumably even the latter build on thought:

In so far as a work becomes eloquent, it manifests either manner or style. Here again the distinction is quantitative, manner being a greater confinement of formal resources and Symbolic ramifications. . . . Manner obviously has the virtue of 'power', with the danger of monotony (Wilde's *Salome* may illustrate both). Style has the virtue of 'complexity', with the danger of diffusion. (The later prose of James Joyce is a good instance of style impaired by diffusion.)[2]

Such a distinction between uneloquent statements, manner and style would be impossible to establish merely by linguistic description. Another, somewhat similar, frame is set up by Paul Goodman in *The Structure of Literature*:

1. Quoted from Joseph T. Shipley, ed., *Dictionary of World Literary Terms*, London, 1955, p. 398.
2. Los Altos, Calif., 1953, pp. 166–7.

Mostly in the sonnets of Milton there is no style; it is the speech of earnestness personally involved and calls all attention to the thought and feeling. Given a similar theme treated by Donne, for instance, much would have to be said about the style; or, in speaking of *Paradise Lost* or *Lycidas*, we should say independent things about the style, as we did in discussing the verses of Catullus. We can speak of 'no style' in three senses: the sense of Milton's sonnets, where a powerful diction is artistically neutralized in the interest of the thought and feeling, and this neutralizing itself is then expressive of attitude; the sense of a nonliterary writing, where the writer has never gotten into contact with his speech—this is 'no style' absolutely; and the sense of poor poetry, where 'no style' is a confusion of styles.[1]

To say that Milton had no style when writing sonnets and that in non-literary writing poor writers never get into contact with their speech will of course necessitate a very personal, complex definition of style, writing and speech. Mr Goodman is hardly helpful when he defines style in his Glossary (p. 276) as 'character of implications'. It is easier to follow De Quincey, who insisted in his essay on language that style may have an independent value apart from the content, and that it may perform either an absolute or a ministerial function:

It is certain that style, or (to speak by the most general expression) the management of language, ranks amongst the fine arts, and is able therefore to yield a separate intellectual pleasure quite apart from the interest of the subject treated . . .[2]

In separating an outer halo of style from an inner core of thought, content or styleless language, and in thus postulating the existence of prelinguistic thought or prestylistic expression, these definitions recall the classic distinction between logic and rhetoric. They also build on the Platonic critics' view of style as a quality that need not be present in every utterance. However, to a student of language, such attempts at defining style are awkward on at least two counts. As the complete, finished text usually is the only reliable means we have of getting at a writer's thought, there seems to be no way of separating the original thought or nascent,

1. Chicago, 1954, p. 215.
2. M, X, 260, quoted by John E. Jordan in *Thomas E. Quincey. Literary Critic*, Berkeley and Los Angeles, 1952, p. 36.

underlying expression from its final verbal garb. Also it becomes impossible to distinguish between utterances that have a style and utterances that do not without employing either completely arbitrary criteria or complex, predominantly subjective ones of a kind that a linguist tries to avoid.

Definitions of style as an addition can be further subgrouped according to which effect of the addition is stressed in each definition. Like many rhetoricians, Stendhal regarded style as effective presentation. Others have more explicitly opposed style to a dry and scholarly recapitulation of facts. Charles Bally's famous theory of style identifies it with a layer of affective elements. According to Bally, stylistics studies

la valeur affective des faits du langage organisé, et l'action réciproque des faits expressifs qui concourent à former le système des moyens d'expression d'une langue.[1]

To Bally, language is a set of means of expression which are simultaneous with thought. A speaker can give his thoughts an objective, intellectual form which conforms to reality as closely as possible. More often, however, he chooses to add various affective elements that partly reflect his ego and partly the social forces he is subject to.[2] The task of stylistics is to examine these *caractères affectifs*, to study the means by which language expresses them and their mutual relations, and to analyse the total *système expressif* of which they are parts:

La stylistique étudie donc les faits d'expression du langage organisé au point de vue de leur contenu affectif, c'est-à-dire l'expression des faits de la sensibilité par le langage et l'action des faits de langage sur la sensibilité.[3]

---

1. *Traité de stylistique française*, Heidelberg, 1921, I, 1. [. . . the affective value of the features of organized language and the reciprocal action of the expressive features that together form the system of the means of expression of a language.—*My translation. N.E.E.*]

2. *Ibid.*, I, 12.

3. *Ibid.*, I, 16. [Consequently, stylistics studies the features of organized language from the point of view of their affective content, that is, the expression of sensibility through language and the effect of language on sensibility.—*My translation. N.E.E.*]

Bally further distinguishes between internal stylistics, which studies the balance and contrast of affective *versus* intellectual elements within one and the same language, and external or comparative stylistics, which compares such features of one language with those of another.[1]

To Bally, then, the origin of style is the addition of a *contenu affectif* to expression. If we substitute emotional content, *Gemüthaftigkeit*, for Bally's affective content, and start from the reader rather than from the writer, we arrive at the definition proposed by Herbert Seidler in *Allgemeine Stilistik*:

Stil ist die durch die Sprache erwirkte, bestimmt geartete Gemüthaftigkeit eines Sprachwerks.[2]

Seidler distinguishes between *Sachdarstellung* and *Sprachkunst*, the latter being characterized by *Gemüthaftigkeit* and thus by style. He admits that style can be present also in *Sachdarstellung*, but only when *das Gemüthafte*, the emotional factor, forms the structural core (*Strukturkern*) of a work can we speak of *Sprachkunstwerke*. Stylistics thus become 'die Wissenschaft vom Stil oder von den Gemütskräften der Sprache.'[3]

A modern version of the very frequent view of style as choice is that of Cleanth Brooks and Robert Penn Warren: '. . . in this book [*Understanding Fiction*], style is used merely to refer to the selection and ordering of language.'[4] Less sophisticated definitions

1. *Le langage et la vie*, Paris, 1926, p. 88.

2. Göttingen, 1953, p. 61. [Style is a definite emotional effect achieved by linguistic means in a text.—*My approximate translation. N.E.E.*]

3. *Ibid.*, p. 65. When I quoted this passage in a lecture, a learned German listener volunteered the wry comment that the virtue of *Gemüthaftigkeit* lies in its being a *Gummiwort*: it stretches without breaking!

4. New York, 1943, p. 605. The definition in *Understanding Poetry*, New York, 1950, p. 640, will do better justice to the views held by the authors: 'This term [style] is usually used with reference to the poet's manner of choosing, ordering, and arranging his words. But, of course, when one asks on what grounds certain words are chosen and ordered, one is raising the whole problem of form. Style, in its larger sense, is essentially the same thing as form.' A large

15

of this type may fall into the same trap as those which regard style as an addition by referring more explicitly to prelinguistic thought. To speak about selection readily leads to an undesirable emphasis on the mental processes of the writer. By the time the reader sees the text, the process of selection is a *fait accompli* only accessible through textual analysis. If the use of 'selection' is merely a roundabout way of referring to features actually present in the text, we might as well try to describe these features directly. And if by 'selection' we are only implying that no writer can use all the resources of his language at the same time, the argument is, at this level of study, trivial. The 'ordering' of language, on the other hand, involves grammatical and literary considerations as well as stylistic ones, and therefore seems too inclusive.

Even if we approve of the idea of style as choice, if we define 'selection and ordering' only with reference to a given text, and thus escape undue emphasis on the mental processes of the writer, we must still accept the onus of distinguishing between different types of choice that are manifested in language. This is a fundamental point sometimes overlooked. One such type is exemplified in the choice between, say, *to eat* and *John* for x in x *loves Mary*. Such a choice is primarily grammatical: *to eat loves Mary* is not English, that is, it does not conform to the patterns occurring in materials that grammarians approve as a basis for descriptions of

---

collection of definitions of style as choice can be readily compiled. See e.g. J. Marouzeau, *Précis de stylistique française*, Paris, 1946, p. 10: 'La langue serait ainsi le catalogue des signifiants et de leurs rapports au signifié représentée par l'inventaire que fournit le dictionnaire et la systématisation que constitue la grammaire. Répertoire des possibilités, fonds commun mis à la disposition des usagers, qui l'utilisent selon leurs besoins d'expression en pratiquant le choix, c'est-à-dire le style, dans la mesure où le leur permettent les lois du langage.' [Language would thus be a catalogue of linguistic symbols and of their connexions with things-meant, represented by the inventory furnished by the dictionary, and by the systematization that is given by grammar. It is a repertory of possibilities, a common stock at the disposition of the users, who use it according to their needs of expression in making the choice—that is, style— within the limits granted to them by the laws of language.—*My translation. N.E.E.*]

English structure.[1] In Marouzeau's words, it is not permitted by the laws of the language. Another type may be illustrated by the choice between *Peter* and *John* in *x loves Mary*, or between *drizzling* and *pouring* in *it was x*. *Peter loves Mary, John loves Mary, it was drizzling* and *it was pouring* are all grammatically possible, but presumably the speaker will, on extralinguistic grounds of truth, prefer one to the other in a given situation. Such a choice will here be called non-stylistic. A third type of selection appears in the choice between *fine man* and *nice chap* in *he is a x*. Both are grammatically possible, even idiomatic; and both have a certain range of frames and referents in common. This type of choice may be labelled as stylistic. It is important to note that stylistic choice exists on a number of different levels, not only in the lexis. It may involve phonetic features (special voice quality, speech rate, &c.), phonemes (*singing/singin'*), morphemes (*sings/singeth*), words, phrases, clauses, sentences, and larger units.

It is, then, necessary for a definition of style as choice to distinguish between these three types of selection: grammatical, non-stylistic, and stylistic. The boundary between grammatical choice and the two other types need here give us little trouble.[2]

1. I am here very crudely cutting a Gordian knot. In applied linguistics, such rough operational procedures are justifiable; there are other areas in which the question of grammaticalness must be approached with great care. For those working with generative grammar, 'grammaticality' is a crucial problem probably best solved in terms of different levels of grammaticalness. See Noam Chomsky, *Syntactic Structures*, 's-Gravenhage, 1957, 2.2–4; Thomas A. Sebeok, ed., *Style in Language*, Boston, Mass., New York and London, 1960, pp. 84–85, 91–92, and 340; Archibald A. Hill, 'Grammaticality,' *Word*, XVII, 1961, 1–10; and Chomsky, 'Some Methodological Remarks on Generative Grammar,' *Word*, XVII, 1961, 219–39.

2. In many countries, schoolteachers notoriously spend much time in deciding whether a given mistake in a student's paper should be penalized more severely as a grammatical mistake, or less severely as an unidiomatic or awkward construction. The solution usually has more to do with the details of the particular syllabus than with questions of linguistic principle: what goes against the recommendations of the grammar-book in use is by definition regarded as a grammatical mistake. Such a scholastic procedure often puzzles the detached outsider who has a better mastery of the foreign language than of local grammar-books.

Briefly, grammar distinguishes between the possible and the im-possible, whereas non-stylistic and stylistic choice both involve grammatically optional selection in that they choose between different, grammatically permissible alternatives. The foreign-language teacher bent on giving his pupils a sense for the style of set texts may assume that these texts are grammatical. Otherwise they would not have been selected for teaching. Besides, in some classroom situations it does not much matter whether a given construction is commented on under the express heading of style or of grammar, as long as the teacher knows exactly what he is doing. Indeed, traditional grammar of the normative kind is full of overlaps between stylistic and grammatical considerations. Friedrich Kainz has labelled this overlap as an example of the general principle of multiple precautions:

Grosse Verstösse gegen die Sprachrichtigkeit wirken im Sinne des Fechnerschen Assoziationsprinzips immer auch hässlich, und eine auf Schönheit Anspruch erhebende Sprachgestaltung wird—von gelegentlichen dichterischen Frei-heiten abgesehen—immer auch die Forderungen der Richtigkeit erfüllen müssen. Die Scheidung zwischen diesen beiden Wertprinzipien und Norm-bereichen wird nur dadurch verwischt, dass die populäre Stilistik ständig mit Wertverschiebungen arbeitet: Sprachgestaltungen, die in schönheitlicher Hinsicht indifferent sind und nur die Klarheit der logischen Fügung beein-trächtigen, werden als hässlich hingestellt; umgekehrt werden Verstösse gegen bestimmte ästhetische Forderungen (den Ausdruckswechsel, z.B.) auch noch dadurch verpönt, dass ad hoc eine grammatische Regel aufgestellt und der lediglich ästhetisch misswertige Verstoss zum Ueberfluss auch noch als Fehler hingestellt wird. Das Prinzip der mehrfachen Sicherung ist ja auch aus anderen Sachbereichen bekannt.[1]

1. *Psychologie der Sprache*, IV, Stuttgart, 1956, 344. [In the sense of Fechner's principle of association, serious violations of linguistic correctness always seem ugly, and—except for occasional instances of poetic licence—an utterance that claims to be beautiful must also satisfy the demands of correctness. The distinc-tion between these two evaluation principles and norm fields is made unclear only by the fact that popular stylistics constantly works with shifts in values. Thus utterances that are aesthetically indifferent and trespass merely against logical clarity are described as ugly, whereas violations of definite aesthetic requirements (such as variation) are additionally penalized by setting up a

The borderline between non-stylistic and stylistic selection is much harder to draw, both being in a sense optional. As an example of choice involving larger units I might quote a text I saw in an Edinburgh hotel-room. The meter that swallowed coins for the electric fire bore a small metal plaque inscribed SHILLINGS ONLY. On the wall there was another plaque giving the management's version: 'Visitors are respectfully informed that the coin required for this meter is 1/-. No other coin is suitable.' Now contemplation of the three types of choice may suggest that the selection between SHILLINGS ONLY and the management's elaborate, but no more informative, politeness is an instance of stylistic choice. It cannot be grammatical, as both utterances satisfy the patterns of English structure, and it cannot be non-stylistic because both utterances exhort the visitor to do, and to abstain from, the same things in the same situation. Stylistic choice, then, at first sight seems to be a choice between items that mean roughly the same, whereas non-stylistic choice involves selection between different meanings. In fact, definitions of style have been based on this observation:

Good style, it seems to me, consists in choosing the appropriate symbolization of the experience you wish to convey, from among a number of words whose meaning-area is roughly, but only roughly, the same (by saying *cat*, for example, rather than *pussy*).[1]

Or, if the choice is tacitly transferred from the writer to the reader, and the reader is given the job of deciding what utterances mean roughly the same:

Roughly speaking, two utterances in the same language which convey approximately the same information, but which are different in their linguistic structure, can be said to differ in style.[2]

---

grammatical rule *ad hoc* and by describing the aesthetically deficient violation as a mistake as well. The principle of multiple precautions is of course also known from other fields.—*My translation. N.E.E.*]

1. Jeremy Warburg, 'Some Aspects of Style' in Randolph Quirk and A. H. Smith, eds., *The Teaching of English*. Studies in Communication 3, London, 1959, p. 50. However, style does not only involve words but other linguistic units as well.

2. Charles W. Hockett, *A Course in Modern Linguistics*, New York, 1958, p. 556.

Such definitions are highly useful and help to clarify an important point. But there is, unfortunately, no simple way of measuring whether the information carried by two different utterances is approximately the same or not. To me, Professor Hockett's examples *Sir, I have the honor to inform you* and *Jeez, boss, get a load of dis* immediately evoke two so different situations and contexts that I should hesitate before regarding their information as approximately the same. (The situations evoked by these two linguistic stimuli must be regarded as part of the information they carry.) A 'meaning-area' is also difficult to determine. Even if we do so by semantic-field techniques, we must in practice start by listing all the contexts in which the items involved occur. It would therefore be simpler to focus directly on context than to appeal to meaning. And if we approach meaning through referents or things-meant, we are again moving from rigorous linguistics into extralinguistic territory. Several types of context are easier to define and classify than things-meant.

Altogether, even if we allow that roughly the same information can be transmitted by different selections of language, we shall find it hard to decide when the information of two utterances is sufficiently similar to permit our labelling the difference between these utterances as stylistic. What about *It is pouring* and *It is raining cats and dogs*? Do they mean the same or not? To what extent a writer is free to choose between grammatically optional elements, and to what extent the same meaning can be conveyed by different linguistic structures readily turn into metaphysical problems beyond the reach of simple and rigorous methods. Indeed Flaubert and many others, including the New Critics, have maintained that there is only one *mot juste*. If this is so, style becomes part of meaning, and two stylistically different utterances can never mean exactly the same. Deciding whether they mean more or less the same is hardly a satisfactory basic operation in investigations of style.

The definition of style as choice, then, leads to problems whose stringent resolution is difficult. I shall return to this question later.[1]

1. See pp. 35 ff. below.

Le style, c'est l'homme même, said Buffon. The epigrammatic elegance of his definition has contributed to its vogue, even at the expense of the finer distinctions and qualifications he made in the same Academy Address in 1753. This emphasis on the individual element of style is, of course, very important, and must be allowed for in all stylistic analysis. As everybody knows, many writers, including a host of great ones, have arrived at the kind of individuality that makes it possible for an experienced reader to identify their writings. Sometimes scholars succeed in doing so by objective means, for example by statistical counts of frequencies of linguistic features in limited contexts.[1] Usually we do so more or less intuitively with the aid of a complex of criteria enclosed in what a scientist might call a black box. The contents of this black box may at first glance defy simple operational description.

The same insistence on the individual quality of style can be found in a vast number of definitions. Here is one of Rémy de Gourmont's:

Avoir un style, c'est parler au milieu de la langue commune un dialecte particulier, unique et inimitable et cependant que cela soit à la fois le langage de tous et le langage d'un seul.[2]

A related concept is that of Pierre Naert,[3] who ascribes style to the Saussurian level of *parole,* not *langue,* just as de Gourmont con-

1. See for instance G. Udny Yule, 'On Sentence-Length as a Statistical Characteristic of Style in Prose,' *Biometrika,* XXX, 1939, 363–90, and *The Statistical Study of Literary Vocabulary,* Cambridge, 1944; Gustav Herdan, *Language as Choice and Chance,* Groningen, 1956 and *Type-Token Mathematics,* 's-Gravenhage, 1960; Alvar Ellegård, *A Statistical Method for Determining Authorship,* Gothenburg Studies in English 13, Gothenburg, 1962, and *Who Was Junius?* Stockholm &c., 1962; Pierre Guiraud, *Les Caractères statistiques du vocabulaire,* Paris, 1954, and Guiraud *et al., Bibliographie critique de la statistique linguistique,* Utrecht, 1954; and below, p. 41, note.

2. *La culture des idées,* Paris, 1916, p. 9. [Having a style means that in the midst of the language shared with others one speaks a particular, unique and inimitable dialect, which is at the same time everybody's language and the language of a single individual.—*My translation. N.E.E.*]

3. *Stilen i Vilhelm Ekelunds essayer och aforismer,* Lund, 1949.

trasts *le langage d'un seul* with *le langage de tous*. In Professor Naert's frame, stylistics is, very elegantly, *la linguistique de la parole* as opposed to *la linguistique de la langue*.

Such definitions are useful enough in the study of styles of individual writers. Still, the identification of style with individual expression leads to two difficulties. First, some features generally labelled as stylistic are not individual at all. They are shared by groups of varying size. Indeed the lack of individual features may serve as a hallmark of some style categories. In officialese and scientific writing, for instance, the writer often aims at, and succeeds in, complete self-effacement. In a general theory of style—as opposed to the *ad hoc* study of an individual writer—it would run counter to established usage and linguistic expediency to exclude group styles from the heading of style. Such group styles are hard to fit exclusively under *parole* in its basic sense of a specific linguistic act by one individual; they could, it seems, with some justification be included under *langue* as well, and perhaps best within the Hjelmslevian subsection of *usage*.

Secondly, how are we to separate the 'unique and inimitable' features of a given style from among all the other features necessarily present in our text? In Saussurian terms, as *langue* can only be approached through *parole*, what corpus of *parole* should we use in setting up that model of *langue* against which our text is to be matched? Such a matching is inevitable as long as we define stylistics as the study of individual expression or as the linguistics of *parole*: unless we compare *la linguistique de la parole* with *la linguistique de la langue* we cannot define what features only occur in the former, and thus what features are characteristic of style. Obviously, to get at style, the investigator must begin with the laborious task of setting up a corpus of reference to find the norm or norms from which a given text differs. To establish such frames of reference is one of the basic aims of all linguistic and literary education. Many critics seem to take it for granted, thanks to the noiseless workings of their black box. But in the study of a foreign language, and even of our own, we must have much experience before we can safely assert that a given text has a style different from that of a range of other texts. In brief: individual modes of expression form a category too special to give us a general basis for an ideally powerful style definition. The identification of style with the individual element of language tacitly presupposes the setting up of norms of comparison.

With this, we have already entered upon definitions of style as a deviation from a norm, which inevitably overlap the definitions based on individual traits of expression. I need only quote one example:

Med stil i språklig bemärkelse brukar menas varje särskilt språkbruk, som tydligt avtecknar sig mot det allmänna. Närmare skulle stilen kunna bestämmas som det från genomsnittet mer eller mindre avvikande sätt att framställa ett ämne, som betingas av ämnets art, framställningens syfte, läsarens förutsättingar och författarens personlighet.[1]

Such definitions are also very useful, especially if they succeed in defining both the norm and the deviations in concrete, operational terms. However, we must again emphasize what was hinted at in the last paragraph. When defining style, we cannot take for granted a norm defined with the aid of style. If we do so, we are merely moving in a circle.[2] Breaking the circularity by contrasting a given style with the language as a whole is impracticable as well as theoretically undesirable.[3] If the norm is to

1. Erik Wellander, *Riktig svenska*, Stockholm, 1948, p. 18. [Style, in the linguistic sense, usually signifies every special usage clearly contrasted against the general. More closely, style could be defined as that way of presenting a subject which differs more or less from the average and which is motivated by the character of the subject, the purpose of the presentation, the reader's qualifications and the writer's personality.—*My translation. N.E.E.*]

2. See further Sol Saporta, 'The Application of Linguistics to the Study of Poetic Language' in Thomas A. Sebeok, ed., *Style in Language*, Boston, Mass., New York, and London, 1960, especially pp. 82–85.

3. Besides, the language as a whole includes the text under investigation. This may lead to complications in the selection of distributional and statistical criteria for analysis. See below, pp. 38–41.

be defined in operationally meaningful terms, it must be carefully circumscribed. But drawing its boundaries is a crucial step which will determine the results of the comparison. To give a crudely obvious instance: if a poet's style is compared with that of an engineering handbook, we are bound to arrive at statements relevant to the difference between poetry and technical prose, not at an assessment of the poet's individuality in terms of the difference between his poems and those of other poets.

Altogether, it seems advisable first to define the norm against which the individuality of a given text is measured, not as the language as a whole but as that part of language which is significantly related to the passage we are analysing. Given the means, we may later return to more ambitious comparisons with a wider range of norms. In the above definition, the subject, the writer's aims, the reader, and the writer's personality were obviously mentioned for this very reason.

Now some norms can be defined with perfect rigour, either by linguistic criteria ('literature in Northumbrian Old English', 'poems written in fourteeners') or with the aid of extra-linguistic context ('third leaders in *The Times* during 1960'). As long as we define the norm so that it yields a meaningful background for the text and feature under analysis, and as long as we limit it with operationally unambiguous procedures, definitions of style as deviations from a norm give us a good first basis for stylistic comparison. In fact the critic's black box was designed precisely to compare the linguistic features of a new text with relevant past experiences of the occurrence of similar linguistic features in related contexts. The crucial point is that limitations of the norm are based on criteria which can be labelled as contextual.

In working towards an increased precision of definitions of style as deviations from a norm, linguists and others have rightly begun to make explicit the rôle of frequencies and of statistical analysis. This enables us to formalize the difference between the usual and the unusual, and between the text and the norm:

The style of a discourse is the message carried by the frequency distributions and transitional probabilities of its linguistic features, especially as they differ from those of the same features in the language as a whole.[1]

Style is defined as an individual's deviation from norms for the situations in which he is encoding, these deviations being in the statistical properties of those structural features for which there exists some degree of choice in his code.[2]

The first of these two definitions again gives us the formidable, and theoretically objectionable, task of using the entire language as a norm. The second involves us in the difficulties inherent in the use of choice as a basis of style.[3] Nevertheless, it seems that if we can only combine the emphasis on frequencies and probabilities with a more precise relationship between text and norm, we shall be on the right track. There is, of course, no risk of the statistician's putting the linguist and the literary critic out of business: in practice, only the linguist and the critic can tell the statistician what features are worth counting in the first place.

As style can be defined as a deviation from a norm, the question arises whether it could be defined positively, in terms of a norm rather than in terms of deviations. We can of course always say that two texts which differ in the same way from a given norm are in the same style. The question is rather, can we do without the norm? We must also distinguish between the definition of style in general and the description of specific style categories. At first sight, the latter seem to yield readily to norm-bound definition, and every literate person is prepared to distinguish a host of norm-defining features in a number of styles. Such features may be stated in terms of metre ('heroic couplets'), time ('Elizabethan style'), place ('Yankee humour'), language, dialect, writer ('Byronic style') or literary work ('Euphuism'), school

1. Bernard Bloch, 'Linguistic Structure and Linguistic Analysis', in Archibald A. Hill, ed., *Report on the Fourth Annual Round Table Meeting on Linguistics and Language Teaching*, Washington, 1953, pp. 40–44.

2. Charles E. Osgood, 'Some Effects of Motivation of Style of Encoding', in Sebeok, ed., *Style in Language*, p. 293.

3. See pp. 15–20 above.

of writers ('romantic style'), genre ('poetic style, journalese'), social situation ('Sergeant-Major of the Guards addressing recruit'), and so forth. Again, all such norms seem to be roughly circumscribed by context, including time, place and situation. And all of them tacitly presuppose definition of a norm. Here, the emphasis is put on similarities, not differences, between the given text and the norm; otherwise this approach is identical with that described above as comparison of the text with a contextually related corpus.

To define style in general in the positive terms of a norm is more difficult. Such attempts have often contained a strongly arbitrary element, and they easily lead to statements such as that quoted on page 13 above, denying Milton's sonnets the privilege of style.

Starting out from Professor Trager's distinction between microlinguistics, viz. the area beginning with phonemes and ending with sentences, and macrolinguistics, concerned with units beyond the sentence, Professor Hill has defined stylistics as concerning

all those relations among linguistic entities which are statable, or may be statable, in terms of wider spans than those which fall within the limits of the sentence.[1]

This definition neither conflicts with the view of style as choice or as tabulation of alternatives, nor rules out the study of frequencies and probabilities as style determinants. Yet it seems to need some explanatory corollaries. Even in phonemic analysis the search for certain types of contrasts may involve spans wider than a sentence: if, for instance, a speaker marks what in writing would be the end of a paragraph with a deeper fall of intonation and a longer pause than the end of a sentence, we may ask whether such devices qualify as entirely stylistic. Also some

1. Archibald A. Hill, *Introduction to Linguistic Structures*, New York, 1958, pp. 406–9.

matters of intersentence concord or selection (*My brother is eight. He/she/it goes to school every day.*) involve spans longer than the sentence, but are nevertheless not stylistic but grammatical. Conversely, there are stylistic matters that are statable within the sentence span (*They said singin', which we found ugly, because we had been taught to say singing*), though here admittedly the morphemics of *singin'/singing* only acquire stylistic significance when viewed in the light of a norm longer than one sentence. If, then, the definition could be amended so as to point out that the longer-than-sentence span concerns the norm rather than the individual stylistic feature under analysis, these explanatory corollaries might perhaps be dispensed with.

4

So far I have hinted at the reasons why style is important in applied linguistics, very briefly glanced at the history of stylistics, especially in terms of the distinction between linguistic and literary subjects, and listed a number of approaches to the definition of style. I shall now attempt a concise summary of a number of relevant principles, concepts, and definitions. To repeat: as my first concern is with applied linguistics, I am here more interested in outlining procedures leading to an ultimately practical view of style and method of stylistic analysis than in building up a complete linguistic theory out of a perfect, logical progression of postulates.

The arrangement of the argument will be simple: I shall start with a definition, and see where it takes us.

First, then, a working definition of style must be attempted. Bearing in mind the objections to the definitions rehearsed in the first half of this monograph, I shall start out from the following statement, whose justification appears above in section 3:

> The style of a text is a function of the aggregate of the ratios between the frequencies of its phonological, grammatical and lexical items, and the frequencies of the corresponding items in a contextually related norm.

Familiarity with frequencies of linguistic items in given contexts is part of the linguistic experience we have acquired ever since childhood. When this past experience is turned to the analysis of a running text, whether heard or read, it is transmuted into a complex flow of expectations which are either fulfilled or disappointed. In stylistic analysis, then, past contextual frequencies change into present contextual probabilities, against whose aggregate the text is matched.

The word 'probabilities' thus includes automatic reference to a relevant norm conditioned by past experience. This leads us to a brief definition:

> The style of a text is the aggregate of the contextual probabilities of its linguistic items.

Two terms, *aggregate* and *contextual*, still need a word of explanation. Style is the *aggregate* of frequencies of linguistic items in two different senses. First, style is the result of more than one linguistic item. For instance, a given word in a text only acquires stylistic significance by juxtaposition with other words. Therefore uncontextualized statistics on single items are of no stylistic significance. Texts longer than one sentence are involved at least in the norm. Secondly, the study of style must not be restricted to phonological or morphological or lexical or syntactic observations: it must be built up of observations made at various levels. Otherwise style merely turns into a sub-department of one of the established steps of linguistic analysis.[1] For example, in a scientific paper on *lepidoptera*, certain zoological terms will be found to have

1. See Martin Joos, 'The Isolation of Styles' in *Georgetown University Monograph Series on Languages and Linguistics* 12, Washington, D.C., 1960, pp. 109–10.

high frequencies; in another scientific paper on molluscs, these zoological terms related to butterflies may have low or zero frequencies; still the style of the two papers may be much the same, which only appears when the aggregate of data from levels other than the technical part of the lexis is brought into the comparison, and when both papers are compared with a contextually different norm.

Style is concerned with frequencies of linguistic items in a given context, and thus with *contextual* probabilities.[1] To measure the style of a passage, the frequencies of its linguistic items of different levels must be compared with the corresponding features in another text or corpus which is regarded as a norm and which has a definite contextual relationship with this passage. For the stylistic analysis of one of Pope's poems, for instance, norms with varying contextual relationships include English eighteenth-century poetry, the corpus of Pope's work, all poems written in English in rhymed pentameter couplets, or, for greater contrast as well as comparison, the poetry of Wordsworth. Contextually distant norms would be, e.g., Gray's *Anatomy* or the London Telephone Directory of 1960.

An appeal to context here obviates the need for references to extralinguistic meaning; the context of a given text is presumably better accessible to objective, linguistic and sociolinguistic classification. Contextual relationships can be defined in many ways. Each text and each passage partakes of several contexts. Some of them are definable in formal, linguistic terms ('last couplet of a Shakespearean sonnet', 'text in rhymed pentameter couplets'). Others involve provenance, period and literary genre. Others must be based on context of situation, including the

1. The relationship between style and context appears, e.g., in Rolf Pipping, *Språk och stil*, Stockholm, 1940, where style is, under the influence of Sir Alan Gardiner's *Theory of Speech and Language* and Ph. Wegener's *Untersuchungen über die Grundfragen des Sprachlebens*, 1885, defined as a result of the speaker/writer's relationship with his public, subject, and linguistic inventory (p. 98).

speaker, the listener, and their relationship and environment. In a study of Mr Micawber's conversation with David Copperfield, one relevant contextual aspect is 'gentleman speaking to a boy'.[1]

Contexts, then, must be defined on several levels, and contextual components can be further classified into various, elaborate patterns.[2] To classify all categories of context *a priori* is impossible, not least because contexts vary from one language, culture and time to another.[3] All we can attempt is 'a limited theory of selection by sociophysical setting',[4] and we must be prepared to revise this limited theory to keep it up to date as changes in our modes of life suggest new, significant context categories. Such new categories often invite projection into the past as well; thus our constant revaluation of old literary texts may partly depend on recent shifts in context classification. Very tentative illustration is therefore the only purpose of lists of features in the contextual spectrum, such as this:

textual context
   linguistic frame
      phonetic context (voice quality, speech rate, &c.)

---

1. In a working paper on 'Applied Linguistics in the Teaching of English as a Secondary Language' read at the Anglo-American Conference on English Teaching Abroad at Jesus College, Cambridge, in June, 1961, Mr J. C. Catford defines 'registers' as 'sub-varieties of dialect (or idiolect) which correlate with the social rôle being played by the performer: e.g. one and the same individual may function socially as, say, a husband/father, as a member of a political party, as a professor of Zoology, &c., and he makes use of a range of *registers* appropriate to these different rôles.' Within the framework of the present essay, registers turn into a sub-variety of style.

2. On such classifications, see e.g. J. R. Firth, *Papers in Linguistics*, London, 1957, pp. 35–36, and Kenneth L. Pike, *Language in Relation to a Unified Theory of the Structure of Human Behavior*, Glendale, Calif., 1954–60, I.5, 52–55 and III.17.

3. In the second part of this book, Spencer and Gregory recognize five major dimensions for placing a text: history, dialect, and field, mode and tenor of discourse.

4. I quote from Jerrold J. Katz and Jerry A. Fodor, 'The Structure of a Semantic Theory', *Language*, XXXIX, 1963, p. 181.

phonemic context
morphemic context (*he sings/he singeth*)
syntactic context (including sentence length and complexity)
lexical context
punctuation, capitalization
compositional frame
    beginning, middle or end of utterance, paragraph, poem, play, &c.
    relationship of text to surrounding textual portions
    metre, literary form, typographical arrangement
extratextual context
period
type of speech, literary genre
speaker/writer
listener/reader
relationship between speaker/writer and listener/reader in terms of sex, age, familiarity, education, social class and status, common stock of experience, &c.
context of situation and environment
gesture, physical action
dialect and language

If items from this list, such as certain phonetic features or gesture, are included in the description of those linguistic features whose contextual spread we wish to study, they must of course be omitted from among the contextual features.

In the quest for meaningful norms of comparison, the first common-sense approach might be based on a question such as: 'With what texts, what types of communication and what responses occurring in what situations should the text or passage we wish to analyse be compared and contrasted in the first place?' In theory our answer will depend on the level of delicacy[1] we wish to aim at in our linguistic description of stylistic elements and in our grouping of contexts; in practice we must be prepared to give it *ad hoc*. The contextual elements must also be fitted into a hierarchy, whose most meaningful arrangement depends on the problem at hand. Roughly speaking, more inclusive contextual groupings are correlated with more comprehensive style categories.[2]

1. See below, p. 39, n. 1.   2. See below, pp. 38–43.

A thorough study of style should be built on the examination of texts that have a number of intersecting contextual relationships. Two questions are relevant here. First, what expressions are used in a given context? Secondly, in what contexts does a given expression occur? We should thus not only look into the differences between, say, conversational passages in Dickens and in Thackeray. We should also see in what situations a given expression occurs in their works (and also in, say, modern English, presuming that the expressions of nineteenth-century novelists ought to be compared with modern idiom).

As the writer is here regarded as part of the context of what he writes, our definition will include all those stylistic elements that consist of personal idiosyncrasies and that constitute a stylistic idiolect.

According to this view, every passage has a constellation of contexts as well as a style. There is no styleless language. 'John is a boy', for instance, contrasts with the logician's 'John is a young male human' and with the doctor's 'John, ♂, 8 yrs'. All three are likely to appear in different contextual constellations. 'Please pass the salt' similarly contrasts stylistically with 'please give me ten milligrams of sodium chloride', which is likely to appear in a related, but different, situational context. In both sentences, A wants some salt from B; in the first sentence, he does so at the table, and in the second, in the laboratory. But 'please pass the salt' does not contrast stylistically with 'please pass the pepper', which is likely to occur in exactly the same situational context in the dining-room. In other words, the choice between *salt* and *sodium chloride* is stylistic, and that between *salt* and *pepper* non-stylistic. I shall return to this question on pp. 35–38 below.

In theory one may perhaps justify stylistic comparison of any texts. But these examples suggest that the most practical starting-point for analyses of style may well turn out to be the examination of frequencies of linguistic items in related, but different, contexts. If the contexts are very closely related, we run an initial risk of not finding style behind the pragmatics of our material. If the contextual relationship is very distant, the whole comparison may be too far-fetched to yield anything but trivial results. In other words, the initial comparison of the styles of the two texts becomes more difficult both if the texts are very similar and if they are very different. The difference between two texts may of course also be diachronic: thus the *Authorized Version* and the *Cambridge Bible* invite stylistic comparison not least because their time-bound context is different, even though the language of the 1611 Bible is regarded as part of living English.

Style, then, is a link between context and linguistic form. It follows that contextualization of the material is necessary if the foreign-language student is to acquire a grasp of its stylistic impact.[1]

There are three ways of measuring the predictability of linguistic items in a given context. First there is the classic method of literary critics to rely upon their experience or 'sense of style' when deciding what expressions are common and what expressions are not. Often, however, their assessments of frequencies are inextricably mixed with other considerations. Secondly, the frequencies in each constellation of contexts can be computed directly out of a corpus of texts, for instance with the aid of a computer. The probabilities in different contextual constellations can then be determined with the aid of statistical formulae. Detailed context analysis is a necessary prerequisite of this method. Thirdly, it is possible to give a group of informants a piece of text as a stimulus or frame, and then to ask them what linguistic item or items they expect to occur next to, or near, it.[2] Conversely, one might ask the informants to define the contexts in which a

---

1. In foreign-language teaching on TV, problems of contextualization come dramatically to the fore. See S. Pit Corder, *English Language Teaching and Television*, London, 1960, pp. 44 ff. and *passim*.

2. This method was used by Iván Fónagy in 'Communication in Poetry', *Word*, XVII, 1961, 194–218.

given expression is likely to appear. The number of correct guesses, or fulfilled expectations, gives a rough measure of the relative predictabilities of the items guessed at. This procedure necessitates an initial distinction between grammatical, non-stylistic and stylistic choice as well as some control of contextual factors before it allows an assessment of stylistic predictabilities. In practice, the informants must be carefully screened as to education, experience, and linguistic ability.

One important step is the grouping of linguistic items into those that function as style markers in a given context, and into those whose stylistic function is limited or nil. To recognize style markers, a study must be made of the distribution of linguistic items in different, but related, contexts.

Let us begin with a simple example. If a statement such as *As everybody knows, the earth is flat* is, in twentieth-century English, invariably found in jocular and humorous contexts, never in serious or scientific ones, it does possess stylistic value and might even serve as a style marker. If a person utters or writes it, we can safely predict he will be joking. If, on the contrary, this statement is found in a range of contexts from jocular to seriously scientific, it cannot serve as a style marker. The same applies to features at other levels of the linguistic spectrum. If a slow rate of speech is characteristic of the delivery of sermons, it can be regarded as part of pulpit style. More inclusive analysis may show that it, in fact, marks a more comprehensive style category such as 'solemn, formal public oratory'. To find examples of context-bound lexical elements is too simple to need illustration here.

We may now define style markers as those linguistic items that only appear, or are most or least frequent in, one group of contexts. In other words, style markers are contextually bound linguistic elements. Elements that are not style markers are stylistically neutral. This may be rephrased: style markers are mutually exclusive with other items which only appear in different contexts, or with zero; or have frequencies markedly different from those of such items.[1]

In the light of this, some otherwise meaningless repetitions of linguistic items acquire meaning as style markers. For instance, the swearing and cursing of a soldier introduces a stream of stylistically significant items—'style reminders'—into statements that would otherwise remain more neutral. The origin of slang can be sought in an effort to create and introduce new style markers unavailable in the existing inventory of linguistic items.

The concept of style markers is of course intimately linked with the view of style as choice discussed above on pages 15–20, to which I shall now return by way of a digression. Stylistic choice, it will be seen, involves the choice of style markers, whereas non-stylistic choice involves selection from among stylistically neutral items. All neutral items are capable of occurring in the context at hand and within the style in question. Non-stylistic choice is thus contextually free, stylistic choice contextually bound. In practice, most utterances are composed of style markers as well as of stylistically neutral elements.

Thus, strictly speaking, the definition of style markers makes it superfluous to worry any longer about style as choice: stylistic choice is simply the context-bound use of style markers. By introducing style markers, our initial definition of style as the aggregate of contextual probabilities has sufficed to distinguish between stylistic and non-stylistic selection. Let us all the same discover if we can construct a model of style as choice, if only to see what difficulties we must face in doing so.

For one such model at least, we must, however reluctantly,

1. In 'Styles as Dialects', *Preprints of Papers for the Ninth International Congress of Linguists*, Cambridge, Mass., 1962, Werner Winter writes: 'A style may be said to be characterized by a pattern of recurrent selection from the inventory of optional features of a language. Various types of selection can be found: complete exclusion of an optional element, obligatory inclusion of a feature optional elsewhere, varying degrees of inclusion of a specific variant without complete elimination of competing features.' (p. 214.)

introduce a fourth type of choice: pragmatic selection. By pragmatic choice I here mean the choice of a meaning for an utterance—or of 'something to say'—by extralinguistic motivation. Pragmatic choice thus involves the decision of what a person wants to convey in his linguistic message. In encoding this message, the speaker may use both style markers and stylistically neutral elements. Now the four levels or types of selection—pragmatic, grammatical, stylistic, and non-stylistic—presumably form a sequential hierarchy of one kind or another. One interpretation of the successive phases of selection involved in our style model takes them in this order, and leads to a process illustrated in the diagram facing this page.

Here the speaker/writer and listener/reader are both part of a given context, A. By extralinguistic motivation, the speaker (for short) wants to convey a message to the listener. This message is to begin with encoded grammatically: only grammatical items pass through the first screen, non-grammatical items being caught. Next, the grammatical items are screened stylistically by criteria determined by context A. This second screen passes all stylistically neutral items as well as the style markers bound to context A, but retains all style markers that cannot occur in context A. Only items screened grammatically and stylistically are thus capable of entering into the speaker's style.

What, then, is wrong with this model? It is, to begin with, not based on any psychophysiological considerations nor on any particular, full theory of linguistic description of language as a whole. Also, grammatical choice here occupies a higher hierarchic position than stylistic choice; the order of the two screens must be reversed if we wish to regard grammatical choice as hierarchically subordinate to stylistic, that is context-bound, selection. The grammar screen must then be placed within the context. This happens for example if we allow poetic contexts a grammar of their own, permitting constructions such as Cummings's *he danced his did*. I have here opted for grammatical priority because this situation is more relevant to foreign-

ONE VIEW OF STYLE AS CHOICE

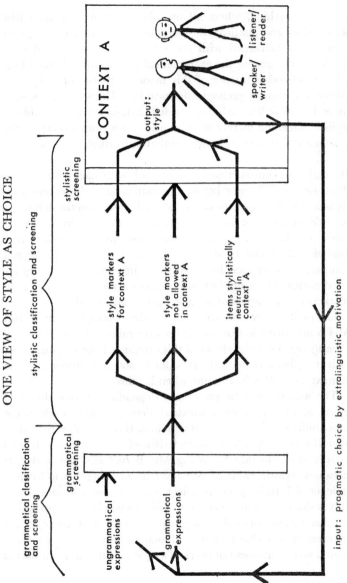

language teaching, where all texts have presumably been first screened by grammatical considerations. (Stylistic screening is of course also concerned with the selection of grammatical style markers from among the grammatically permissible items.) Finally, a debatable feature of this model is its use of pragmatic choice and thus of prelinguistic meaning. The scheme becomes more defensible if we take for granted that, for a given individual, stylistic screening merely involves a selection from among all the grammatical structures known to that individual.

We may thus construct various more or less satisfactory models to illustrate the difference between grammatical, stylistic, and non-stylistic selection. But one of the main advantages in the definition of style as the aggregate of contextual probabilities is that it gives us a chance of bypassing such models in our actual stylistic analysis, which can be directly concerned with the operational comparison of frequencies of linguistic items in contextually related norms. The aim of stylistic analysis is the inventory of style markers and a statement of their contextual spread.

Let us illustrate this with yet another example. Mr N and Mrs N are sitting in front of the fire on a rainy day. N says, *What a beastly day!* Does the choice of this utterance have stylistic value, or is it stylistically neutral? It is, let us note, conditioned by the context 'N to Mrs N at home when it rains'.

The answer may be yes or no, depending on our choice of norms and levels in the contextual hierarchy against which the probability of N's utterance is matched. If we find that the utterance *What a beastly day!* is characteristic of N as opposed to B, who usually reacts to rain by asking Mrs B *Isn't this rain awful?*, it possesses stylistic value at one level by marking N's individual style, or stylistic idiolect, as different from B's on that same level. If it is shared by most members of N's social class, as opposed to another socially definable category of people who use other expressions in a similar context, it functions as a marker of a class-bound style, but does not mark N's style as different from that of others of his own social class. If, again, *What a beastly day!* mostly occurs in N's fireside conversation, not in his shop-talk with other chartered accountants, it is characteristic of his familiar style or register. And so forth.

In spite of the downpour, N might conceivably also have said *What a lovely afternoon!*, presumably if he had a taste for irony. Now if N mostly reacts to rain by calling it *lovely*, whereas B, C, and D mostly call it *beastly*, this also separates N's individual style from those of B, C, and D. But N's individual taste for irony will not have sufficient weight to characterize the style of N, B, C, D and their peers as a group. The study of group usage naturally necessitates study of more than one informant.

Similar phenomena can be found in literary texts as compared with norms circumscribed by literary contexts. The interesting point is that in all these comparisons, the same linguistic element may appear as a style marker when matched against one norm, and as stylistically neutral when compared with another. This may lead to initial confusion. The general resolution of such problems must be sought in hierarchic levels of contexts and context-bound norms, and thus in the delicacy[1] of the analysis. As always, maximally delicate statements are meaningless because they merely reproduce the primary data in full. Therefore no stylistic analysis should start by studying linguistic behaviour in terms of absurdly detailed, transitory, and unique contextual constellations. We have to climb to higher rungs on the hierarchic ladder of contexts before we arrive at meaningful descriptions of styles.

So, when matched against the very low-level and delicate norm of 'Mr B to his wife at home when it rains', Mr N's use of

1. I have borrowed this extremely useful concept from Dr M. A. K. Halliday's article 'Categories of the Theory of Grammar,' *Word*, XVII, 1961, p. 268, where it is defined as 'depth of detail' and as a 'cline running from a fixed point at one end (least delicate, or 'primary') to that undefined but theoretically crucial point (probably statistically definable) where distinctions are so fine that they cease to be distinctions at all, like a river followed up from the mouth each of whose tributaries ends in a moorland bog.'

What a beastly day! is stylistic if (*a*) it is contextually bound (for instance, provoked by rain), and (*b*) it has a much greater frequency in N's speech than in that of B. However, if we match N's utterance against higher, less delicate and more inclusive norms such as 'middle-class husbands to their wives' or 'middle-class people in familiar conversation', such frequency differences are likely to disappear as we stop paying attention to minute contextual details (in this case, rain) and simultaneously increase the range of the norm. But if N's *What a beastly day!* is matched against the frequencies in sermons, and if it proves to have a very low frequency in sermon contexts, it will have stylistic significance in marking N's fireside conversation as different from sermons. The linguistic description of utterances in stylistic analysis should similarly aim for suitable delicacy levels. Thus *What a beastly day!* can, at one such level, be regarded as a sentence with the intonation contour of an exclamation and with the structure *what a* + one of the adjectives *beastly, lovely, gorgeous, terrible, nasty, horrid*, &c., + substantive. It will of course be more meaningful to look for instances of this whole class of expressions than merely for the one sentence *What a beastly day!* All this, incidentally, agrees with common-sense views of style.

The norm, then, should be chosen so as to have a meaningful contextual relationship with the text whose style we are studying. The higher we climb on the hierarchic ladder of styles in our choice of contexts and levels of comparison, the fewer are the stylistic choices, the fewer the style markers, the larger and more inclusive the style categories, and the more numerous the stylistically neutral choices and items. Therefore the delicacy of stylistic analysis—as indeed of all linguistic analysis—should be set at the level providing us with optimally meaningful results. If we go too high, for instance by defining the norm in terms of the language as a whole, we lose significant details; if we aim too low, we fail to see the forest for mere trees. All this should once again remind us of the importance of basing stylistic analyses on adequate materials, and of thus avoiding the excessively delicate—as well as excessively far-fetched—approaches warned against in section 4 above.

To sum up: after the style markers in a sufficiently large number of texts have been compared with those in a sufficiently large number of suitably selected norms, and after the contextual ranges have been correspondingly widened, it becomes possible to formulate increasingly general and powerful descriptions of styles and style categories. We are then advancing along the cline from more delicate to less delicate statements, and gradually working up from the analysis and description of individual passages, texts and substyles to the determination of more inclusive categories of style.

Style being a matter of frequencies, not only of occurrence *versus* non-occurrence, absolute mutual exclusion is not the only distributional pattern with stylistic relevance. Statistical trends too provide us with many style markers.[1] For instance, the choice between active and passive constructions in English is one of those whose stylistic correlations can be expected to appear only, or largely, in statistical terms. As long as both types of construction are grammatical, the choice between them cannot be a matter of grammar. If the use of one or the other is contextually bound, the choice is stylistic. Thus the writer of an adventure story is likely to opt mainly for vigorous active constructions, whereas the scientist will prefer to report on his procedures by effacing his ego behind a passive. But even the scientist may occasionally emerge with a direct first-person sentence. If, on the other hand, the choice is dictated by emphasis (as in *The Christians were eaten by lions* in a text on Christians, not lions), it becomes non-stylistic.

1. See above, p. 21, first footnote; and Werner Winter, *op. cit.*, and especially 'Relative Häufigkeit syntaktischer Erscheinungen als Mittel zur Abgrenzung von Stilarten', *Phonetica*, VII, 1961, 193–216. Several papers in the past few years' files of *Voprosy Jazykoznanija* also present relevant data; see e.g. S. I. Kaufman, 'Ob imennom kharaktere tekhnicheskoje stilja' in X, 1961: 5, 103–8.

This view is justified by the fact that passives occur over a very wide contextual spread in instances where the main subject of the passage would otherwise be hidden as the object of an active construction. The use of the passive for emphasis is therefore not strictly bound contextually. But even if the choice between actives and passives is sometimes non-stylistic, in English a high incidence of passive constructions functions as a very striking style marker. Sentence and clause length, sentence complexity, word length, and a host of other features may also yield statistical trends sufficiently context-bound for the marking of styles. At least in theory, strikingly low frequencies of certain linguistic items may similarly characterize definite style categories.

The style markers that appear in the same text form a stylistic set for that text.

An example. In French we find that texts characterized by one contextual constellation (roughly, 'literary') use the *passé simple* as a narrative tense, mark questions by inversion (*Monsieur votre père vient-il?*), and employ *nous*. Texts characterized by another contextual constellation (roughly, 'colloquial') avoid the *passé simple*; form questions with the aid of tags such as *est-ce que* and, in speech, intonation, but do not invert the word order; and use *on* instead of *nous*, with the verb in the third person singular.[1] In a suitably selected sample of two types of context-determined

1. There is of course no contradiction between the citing of this example (borrowed from André Martinet, *Eléments de linguistique générale*, Paris 1960, pp. 163 and 173) and the insistence on contextual relationship, voiced above. Even if *Monsieur votre père vient-il?* and *Il vient, ton père?* occur in contexts that are different in terms of the polarity between literary and colloquial situations, they have other contextual features in common. Thus both are questions inquiring about the arrival of the conversational partner's father. Comparable examples could be cited from a host of languages. I have, for instance, observed that in my own spoken Finland-Swedish I make a consistent contextual distinction between two styles, one with *skulle* and imperfect forms of the type *kallade*, and another with *sku* and *kalla*. In this instance the polarity is between formal and familiar speech.

texts we shall find that these three items are mutually exclusive and that each text will use either Set I or Set II without mixing items from the two sets:

Set I: *passé simple*, inverted questions, *nous*

Set II: no *passé simple*, non-inverted questions, *on*

Within this sample, we may predict: if we find an instance of *passé simple*, we can expect the same text to have *nous* and inversion in questions, but not constructions such as *Il vient, ton père?* or *on* for the first person plural.

The style markers that are shared by a large number of texts within a range of related but different contexts form a major stylistic set. Those texts that share a major stylistic set belong to the same major style. Analysis of a sufficiently large number of texts covering the entire contextual spectrum of a given language will result in a definition of the major styles of that language. These can be labelled and defined, e.g. with terms that suggest important contextual categories or style markers. Thus in French we might make one major distinction between *passé-simple* style and non-*passé-simple* style. In English, the labels frozen, formal, consultative, casual, and intimate have been suggested for five major style categories.[1] It is worth a passing note that the most classic of all such categorizations—the distinction of three levels, *stylus gravis*, *mediocrus* and *humilis*—may well have owed its success through the centuries to its close links with a literary tradition permitting only three major contextual categories, whose main features could be summarized in Virgil's Wheel.

In many contexts, styles can be expected to overlap. If in a given context different speakers use different styles, which they else-

---

1. Joos, *op. cit.* In 'Entropija russkogo jazyka', *Voprosy Jazykoznanija*, XI, 1962: 6, 115–30, A. A. Piotrovskaja and co-workers distinguish between four major styles in Russian: conversational, belletristic, factual, and poetic. Conversational passages from Nekrasov, Babel, and Grossman come under conversational style.

where agree in associating with the same contextual ranges, this context is stylistically ambiguous. For example, if, in situation A, one educated young man uses the more formal *yes, Sir* and another equally educated young man prefers the less formal *yes*, though there are other situations in which both agree in using either *yes, Sir* or *yes*, situation A is contextually ambiguous. Such overlaps are likely to increase towards the boundaries between the contextual areas of different styles, and may therefore give us clues to contextual and stylistic groupings.

An overlap of stylistic sets[1] within a given passage of text will first of all motivate a critical re-examination of the criteria by which these sets were obtained. If the method was sound, such an overlap is the result either of a mixture of styles, or, if further analysis shows that each set is consistently used in definite portions of the text, of one or several shifts of style.

Many literary effects are based on a shift of style, which may be defined as a switch from one stylistic set to another. In terms of our basic definition of style it involves a shift in the probabilities of the linguistic items of the text as measured against one and the same contextual norm. If, for instance, a clergyman delivering a sermon shifts from biblical idiom into colloquial English, this lowers the probabilities of his linguistic items as matched against biblical and pulpit norms. We might also regard the same change as a norm shift if for some reason we find it more expedient to match the probabilities, no longer against those of biblical English but against those of colloquial usage. But we must still remember the context (here, the pulpit). The intentional or unintentional use of a style marker or a stylistic set in an unambiguously alien context might be labelled as contextual transfer. It can be compared to the wearing of brown shoes with black tie; its effects vary from the striking through the humorous, the awkward and the rude to the disastrous.

A shift of style must not be confused with metaphor. Metaphor

1. That is, stylistic sets already established by study of other texts.

involves collocational shifts at the lexical level under specific semantic constraints, but without regard to such other contextual limitations as enter into style. Of course, given types of metaphors and their frequencies may function as important style markers, not least in poetry. If a given metaphor introduces a word from an alien stylistic set, it also involves a shift of style; if the metaphoric term is taken from the same stylistic set as the rest of the utterance, no shift in style will result.

In many types of texts, such as plays and novels, different passages often use different styles. The style of a narrative passage, for instance, may contrast with that of dialogue or interior monologue. Such shifts of style are obviously accompanied by shifts of context. The same holds true of the speech of different characters, the speaker being part of the context of what he says. Those subvarieties of style which correlate with the varying social rôles of a given speaker or writer may be called registers.

Another distinction that should be kept in mind is that between style and dialect,[1] for instance in works mixing dialects, or dialects and standard language, for literary effect. If dialect is used only in readily definable contexts, it can most conveniently be regarded as a sub-variety of style; a shift of dialect thus turns into a shift of style. So in *Lady Chatterley's Lover*, Mellors's change from Standard English into dialect has obvious connexions with shifts in context and with stylistic features. The frequency of taboo words, for instance, is higher in the dialect passages. Mellors can also be said to employ two major registers, one dialect register and one Standard English register, which may perhaps be further subdivided by more detailed reference to the different social rôles with which his choice of idiom is linked.

There are many instances of situations in which even the choice of language within one and the same society has been

1. See Werner Winter, 'Styles as Dialects', *Preprints of Papers for the Ninth International Congress of Linguists*, Cambridge, Mass., 1962, pp. 214–19.

more or less markedly context-bound. Obvious European examples include the use of Greek in the Roman Empire, of Latin in the Middle Ages and Renaissance, of French in England during the Middle-English period, of Danish in Norway, of Swedish in Finland at least before 1863, and of French among the upper classes of eighteenth-century Europe and pre-revolutionary Russia.

Even if the use of a second language is widespread and consistent enough to be bound by context, it can be dealt with by the principles and methods described above. The distinction between dialect and style can be approached in two ways. Either we define the material subjected to stylistic analysis as dialectally homogeneous and classify possible dialects as varieties of style, or we begin by grouping passages by dialect and proceed to separate stylistic analysis of each of the dialects that occur in our text. It is, however, always relevant to note possible correlations between context and dialect as well as between shift of context and shift of dialect.

One reason complicating a general discussion of style, dialect and language is that traditional distinctions between dialect and language are based on historical and cultural, not purely linguistic, developments and principles. Thus languages and dialects have very different status and prestige in different multilingual and multidialectal environments.

We may further distinguish between microstylistics and macrostylistics. Microstylistics is the study of style markers and stylistic sets within the sentence or within units smaller than the sentence, whereas macrostylistics is the stylistics of sentence sequences.

The study of features not statable in terms of contextual probabilities of linguistic items, style markers, stylistic sets and shifts of style is not the task of stylistics but of other levels of linguistic or literary analysis.

5

AFTER this brief outline of suggestions towards concepts of style theory and principles and procedures of stylistic analysis I shall make some supplementary remarks with more direct bearing on applied linguistics and the foreign student's problems.

As we have seen, style is one of the areas where linguistics, pragmatics, and aesthetics readily overlap. Part of the difficulty in discussing style follows from the temptation to attempt simultaneous answers to linguistic, pragmatic, and aesthetic questions, which are concerned with different levels of, and attitudes to, the communication process. Let us once again remind ourselves that present-day linguistic techniques in the narrow, rigorous sense are focused on descriptions of the linguistic features that occur in a given text, and on analyses of their distribution and frequency. Unlike the linguist, the literary critic regards these linguistic features as one of the sets of stimuli that trigger off a response. He is primarily concerned with descriptions of his own response and of its correlations with the responses of other critics.

It follows that in foreign-language teaching, and indeed in many debates about the essence of style, stylistic analysis can be conveniently approached in terms of two stages or levels or methods, which should all the same be inextricably fused in the classroom. In this paper, the linguistic description, inventory, and distributional as well as statistical analysis of stylistic features will be abbreviated as SL (from stylolinguistics). The study of the correlations between stylistic stimuli and the reader's response will be labelled as SB (from stylobehaviouristics). I have adopted these two abbreviations, SL and SB, precisely because they are arbitrary enough to lack the undesirable and over-restrictive connotations of the unabbreviated terms. (Besides, they are shorter.) Thus SB is not limited to the study of aesthetic responses or of overt gestures. It also includes the study of other types of reactions such as social attitudes to linguistic items and stylistic levels, associations with extratextual contexts, &c.

It must be stressed that the problems studied in SL and SB are all part of the total meaning of the text,[1] though SL and SB focus on different aspects of that meaning. I therefore have no objection to a linguist's regarding SB as disguised SL, or a psychologist's labelling of SL as a mere extension of SB. I still think this distinction is a useful mnemonic device reminding us of the different angles from which style can be viewed.

In SL, various systems of linguistic description can be used. Each of the systems of grammar—the traditional Latinate system,

---

1. It does not, however, follow that semantics, in its technical sense of a theory and a step in linguistic analysis, must include stylistics. Though grammar too is a crucial component in meaning, semantics need not (or, according to some linguists, must not) include grammatical statements. According to Jerrold J. Katz and Jerry A. Fodor ('The Structure of a Semantic Theory', *Language*, XXXIX, 1963, p. 172), indeed 'synchronic linguistic description minus grammar equals semantics'. When fixing an upper boundary for semantics, Katz and Fodor write: 'Previous conceptions of semantics have usually defined the goals of a semantic description of a natural language in such a way that to achieve them semantic theory would have to account for the manner in which settings determine how an utterance is understood. We shall now show that to set the goals of a semantic theory this high is to set them too high. Once we have shown that a semantic theory cannot be expected to account for the way settings determine how an utterance is understood, we will have fixed an upper bound on the domain of semantic theories. That is, we will have shown that a semantic theory is a theory of the speaker's ability to interpret the sentences of his language.' (p. 176.) In fact such a definition draws a very neat boundary between semantics and the contextual view of style proposed here. Apart from the obvious difficulties and hazards of context analysis, one question to worry about is whether the semantics of Katz and Fodor, and our approach to style, are separated by a no-man's land covered by neither.

phoneme-morpheme grammar, system-structure grammar and transformation grammar—may have special advantages absent from the other systems. In teaching in Europe, the traditional categories of Latinate grammar may still be helpful because they are so far best known to the majority of students. They also facilitate some types of basic comparison between one Indo-European language and another (while simultaneously making other comparisons more difficult), and they are closely linked with the literary traditions of the western world. No defence is necessary for other, scientifically more satisfactory types of linguistic description.

In principle, the system of description must be adequate for the analysis of all features that may possess stylistic significance. It is therefore wrong to take for granted that a descriptive apparatus based exclusively on the categories of spoken language is automatically adaptable to the study of written texts, which may carry important features of their own, such as punctuation, paragraph division, typographical arrangements, graphemic devices, special morphological and syntactic constructions, and features of literary traditions lacking in spoken language.[1] In some languages, SL may necessitate the construction of special methods of linguistic description. In others, especially in those with a long literary and grammatical tradition, scholastic grammar and semantics may well prove more adequate for the basic SL of written texts than for rigorous analysis of spoken language.

Like all linguistic description, SL should most conveniently start from the study of a closed text or corpus that can be strictly limited either by linguistic or by unambiguous extralinguistic criteria. It is therefore easiest to begin by analysing the style of one text by comparing it to a restricted norm. One approach to the study of such a corpus is the linguist's usual analysis of the

1. See G. M. Messing, 'Structuralism and Literary Tradition', *Language*, XXVII, 1951, 1–12, and David Abercrombie, 'Conversation and Spoken Prose', *English Language Teaching*, XVIII, 1, 1963.

distribution of features, and here of features that do, or may, have a stylistic rather than a grammatical or pragmatic function; or, in other words, of potential style markers. Its power of prediction —that is, the power of its statements to predict what happens outside the closed corpus on which it was based—depends on the delicacy of the SL, on the size of the material, and on the contextual relationship between the original closed corpus and the open material to which the statements are applied.

SB can be approached either through the written work of critics or through the responses of one or several informants. In the teaching situation mentioned above in the opening section, the typical informant is a foreign university lector or a schoolteacher. Some types of SB seem to be accessible to study by psychological or sociological techniques, including those involving quantification and factor analysis.[1]

The responses set up as models for the language learner must be representative, and their choice involves extralinguistic considerations. Among them are the factors affecting the teaching situation: the level of the students, the competence of the teacher, the aims of the teaching, and the facilities available. Features of the literary tradition and social as well as pragmatic background of the texts are also important; hence my emphasis of *realia* in section 1. The latter can be regarded as part of the material to be taught, and should be chosen with the usual principles of limitation, grading, staging, and presentation in mind.

The aim of the teaching is to make explicit the correlations between SL and SB, and thus to make the students respond to specific stimuli described by SL in a manner determined by models found through SB. Interference from the student's first

1. See Charles E. Osgood, George J. Suci and Percy H. Tannenbaum, *The Measurement of Meaning*, Urbana, Ill., 1957. In 'Criteria for Style Analysis', *Word*, XV, 1959, 165 ff., Mr Michael Riffaterre uses the term 'AR', 'average reader', for a group of informants.

language, social bias and past experience must be reckoned with in the selection of materials and methods.

A talented and well-educated teacher with a good command of the language has a built-in sense of SB conditioned by past experience. This enables him to proceed from SB to SL by seeking out, defining and describing the stimuli that provoked his responses. Nevertheless it is desirable to set up methods for SL that are as independent as possible from SB. This may not be necessary in all classroom situations; but it becomes imperative in all rigorous linguistic analysis of style as well as in all instances where SB is lacking. The latter predicament must be faced in stylistic analyses of languages, such as dead ones, in which no informants are available and in which no texts on grammar, rhetoric, literary criticism and history, biography, and the like give us clues to SL-SB relationships. Under such circumstances the only possible approaches to SB are through SL, and through the extrapolation of observations made from other materials. With what success SB can be reconstructed will of course depend on a large number of factors, whose study is a subject in its own right.

The aim of SL was defined as the linguistic description of stylistic elements; the classroom aim of SB was to study models of approved responses to stylistic stimuli and to give the student approved patterns of stimulus-response behaviour. We may now be a bit more explicit in our suggestions towards methods for SB. As style is determined by contextual probabilities, contexts become a crucial feature to reckon with in the selection and grading of stylistic stimuli. At first, the student's range of stylistic responses must be enlarged by conscious effort involving contextualization, context analysis and possibly explicit rationalization. Responses must always be linked with specific stimuli in context, for instance in a manner resembling that of the New Critics. Empathy, in the sense of the students' projecting themselves into, and adopting, approved responses should be encouraged until they have acquired sufficient experience of contextual probabilities and major styles to be capable of reacting more spontaneously. But controls and examination questions must not be designed to reward mere reproduction of approved statements, at least not longer than absolutely necessary. The teacher should also work out patterns for active drill involving the choice between style markers in context as well as the definition of contexts from style markers. At first blush, such teaching methods may seem much too mechanical to cater for the subtleties of stylistic analysis. All the same, even in their first language, people acquire their sense of style by an educational process involving the acquisition of approved responses to linguistic and literary stimuli. The difference between the untutored native and the language learner in the classroom is that the former has an extensive experience of the probabilities of linguistic items within a certain, though limited, contextual range; the latter must acquire his entire experience through a more or less formalized, controlled, and graded educational process.

It has sometimes been taken as a rough working hypothesis that elements with low probabilities have a greater literary effect than elements with high probabilities. In practice there is a great difference between different schools of writers precisely in their consistency of probability patterns. Thus originality in mediaeval or neoclassical poetry is not the same thing as originality in Metaphysical or modern poetry. The predictability of Pope is different from the predicability of a surrealist poet; one is here reminded of André Breton's principle that the highest aim of poetry is to juxtapose objects as unrelated as possible and *les mettre en presence d'une manière brusque et saisissante*. Further, predictability is also influenced by statistical parameters: in a long poem in a very regular metre, even minor metrical variations may stand out more markedly than in a short, metrically regular poem, not to speak of a metrically less regular work.

At the same time, elements with a high predictability (in other words, utterances very common in their particular context) may have a very strong literary effect, even if their information value in terms of information theory is low or nil. Thus in a tragedy, a perfectly ordinary and predictable conversational response may carry a tremendous emotional charge. In the concluding act of *A Doll's House*, Nora's *Her lægger jeg nøglerne*—'I lay the keys here'—is grammatically, semantically, and stylistically an ordinary, everyday statement. In the play, however, it movingly symbolizes Nora's absolute determination to break with the past. Especially if a literary text is distant in time or place, we may also run the opposite risk of reading emotional values into utterances that had no such emotional charge in their original context. Thus Herodotus' terse conclusion, 'So fought the Hellenes at Thermopylae', might be construed as the noblest possible conclusion for an account of supreme heroism. But a Greek scholar will tell us that Herodotus' words are merely a Greek writer's routine signal for a transition from one subject to another.[1] Such observations are relevant in more than one way. They involve one of the characteristics of language that make the application of information theory to literature so difficult.[2] They also remind us of the difference between two types of literary criticism: that which laboriously reconstructs the time-and-place-bound context of each work, and that which approaches, say, English seventeenth- and eighteenth-century poems from tacitly or explicitly modern canons of language and literary evaluation.

It must therefore be emphasized that style and literary effect— and thus stylistics and literary criticism—are two different things. Every utterance has a style determined by contextual probabilities, but there are many utterances that are poor litera-

1. I owe this example to Albert Wifstrand, *Tider och stilar*, Lund, 1944, pp. 15–16.

2. This is, of course, not to deny that certain types of literature carry more 'information' in the technical sense than certain other types of literature. But the quantity of information need not be correlated with literary values. On the application of information theory to language, see e.g. Colin Cherry, *On Human Communication*, New York and London, 1957, pp. 167–216.

ture. In SB, however, the context-bound literary effects of an utterance may be difficult to keep apart from stylistic effects proper. What efforts are worth making in this direction depends on the teaching situation.

6

To conclude this crowded essay, a few summary comments may be in order.

Style has proved notoriously hard of stringent definition. A linguistic method of stylistic analysis should avoid initial reference to extralinguistic meaning, which is not accessible to rigorous analysis. Thus stylistic selection should not be defined as 'the choice between items that mean more or less the same'.

Here an initial appeal to meaning has been avoided by a tentative definition of style as the aggregate of contextual probabilities. Some classification of contexts is therefore a prerequisite for the present approach to stylistic analysis. Contexts are more directly accessible to observation and operational analysis than the total complex of meaning. Still, there classification must be based on *ad hoc* considerations. A limited theory of sociophysical context is all we can hope to set up *a priori*, and such a theory must be revised in the light of each specific situation. Though the classification of contextual constellations can be carried to any lengths, meaningful results can all the same be obtained with a rough-and-ready limitation of contextual categories.

All stylistic analysis is ultimately based on the matching of a text against a contextually related norm. Such norms may be explicitly circumscribed, or they may remain implicitly embedded in the past experience of a speaker, writer, or literary critic. A reference to context makes possible the definition of a norm without initial reference to style, which still remains unknown at that point of the procedure. The present approach thus avoids the circularity inherent in some theories of style.

Contextually bound linguistic items function as style markers. Style markers occurring in the same text form a stylistic set for that text. A stylistic set shared by a large number of contextually related texts forms a major stylistic set occurring within a major contextual range. Texts sharing the same major stylistic set are in the same major style. Style markers consist of statistical trends or of mutually exclusive items.

Allowance has to be made for different speakers' use of different styles in the same, stylistically ambiguous context. If stylistic sets which have been proved different by previous analyses occur within the same text, we have an instance of one, or several, shifts of style. The use of a stylistic set in an unambiguously alien context may be labelled as contextual transfer.

In practice we should try to avoid both extremes of the delicacy scale in our linguistic description of style markers as well as in our classification of contextual constellations. Excessive delicacy leads to an excessive concern with cumbersome, transitory details and to style classifications lacking in inclusiveness and power. Too little delicacy leads to a loss of stylistically significant features.

The distinction between SL (the linguistic description of stylistic stimuli) and SB (the study of responses to such stimuli) will, I hope, simplify the cross-purpose debate between linguists and literary critics about the essence of style. In foreign-language teaching, the SL-SB relationship involving the acquisition of approved responses to stylistic stimuli deserves much attention.

Once some important contextual groupings, style markers, stylistic sets and major styles have been found and defined, the teacher can draw upon this material in the teaching of style in a foreign language. In many teaching situations, passive recognition and active use of important style markers and stylistic sets may deserve a high priority.

Context analysis is one of the weak links, and probably the weakest, in the approach outlined above. Nevertheless, though the classification of contexts can hardly be rigorous in the most exacting scientific terms, we must not forget that it is more objective than many others in wide and unquestioned use among students of literature, and even of language. It should not, for instance, compare unfavourably with some lexicographical methods that have given valuable results. As long as the suggestions made here will add to, not detract from, the accuracy with which we discuss style, no apologies are indicated. In spite of the self-imposed restrictions that have revolutionized linguistics we should not lose sight of the fact that men, women, and children use language for social purposes and in a sociophysical environment. Unless this sociophysical context is admitted at some level of linguistic analysis, we run the risk of ignoring a crucial aspect of linguistic communication.

There are two fundamentaly different approaches to defining the meanings of well-known and much used linguistic terms. The conservative approach reckons with established usage; the radical approach finds the only virtue in theoretical stringency and internal consistency, and is apt to give old words new, arbitrary and strictly restricted spheres of application. Here, 'style' has been defined fairly conservatively: the result should not depart unduly from accepted common-sense views.

An approach

to the study of style

JOHN SPENCER
MICHAEL GREGORY

1

STYLE in literature is a recognizable but elusive phenomenon. As Nils Erik Enkvist[1] demonstrates, it is a concept which, though widely used and multifariously defined, yet evades precision. This difficulty of precise definition need not, however, lead us to abandon the concept. The same problem arises with many of the abstract, generalized concepts without which neither humanist nor scientist could proceed far in the tasks of analysis, comparison and validation of hypotheses. This is especially so where qualitative evaluations of phenomena are involved: when phenomena cannot easily be quantified, mathematically precise definitions are unlikely to be forthcoming. So it is, to a high degree, with style.

The concept of style is, of course, the product of abstraction. It is abstract in the first place in the sense that style is one quality out of several possessed by any work of literature. A poem, a novel, or an essay is clearly more than its style; of its totality its style is a part. But the concept is also abstract in another sense. Most notions of style carry with them an implication of individuality *vis-à-vis* generality; or, put another way, the matching of unique qualities against qualities shared with other works.

A further important point needs to be observed. If style in literature is the product of a particular, and in part unique, use of language, then it is related to, and dependent upon, certain notions of the proper function of language as a whole. This takes us beyond the realm of literature as such, and involves us in the relation between language use and social and cultural patterns. Only thus are we able to account for notions of style which shift

1. Present volume, pp. 10–27.

and change in different periods and among different groups. Literature can be regarded as part of the total patterning of a culture, as a relatively self-contained 'institution' of that culture; and when literary scholars use the terms 'literary tradition' or 'literary convention' they are, quite appropriately for many purposes, treating literature as just such an 'institution'. This way of viewing literature, however, has its limitations, which need to be recognized: this because the permissible range of reference in literature extends over virtually the whole of a culture. Literature is, at least potentially, fully exoteric. This exotericism of reference is reinforced by the fact that language, the medium of literature, is not confined to literature alone. Indeed, it is the medium which carries the whole of the culture of which the literature is one aspect. This interpenetration of literature, language, and culture makes style, in the final analysis, a cultural phenomenon. And because literature is dependent upon language, which is itself intrinsic to the culture as a whole, the student of style must see language in literature in relation to other functions of language.

This link between the language of literature and language used for other purposes, and the consequent necessity of seeing language used in literature in terms of the language as a whole, means that part of the discussion which follows must be devoted to considering the contribution that can be made to the study of style by the theories, procedures, and attitudes of general and descriptive linguistics, the particular concern of which is the systematic study of the whole of that part of human activity called language. It is difficult to believe that linguistics has no contribution to make in this field; a central concern of this monograph will be with the nature and extent of the contribution. Initially, however, and in place of any endeavour to define style explicitly, there now follows an attempt to see how stylistic qualities and differences in literature are apprehended.

2

THE immediate response to a text which stimulates the literary critic to a detailed examination of it has something in common with the development of scientific theories. The creative intelligence of the literary critic presents, perhaps inchoately at first, a response to a work of literature which is a kind of hypothesis, a basis for further observation and testing. The imagination of both the literary scholar and the scientist is concerned with the same task: the attempt to envisage possibilities that are consonant with reality.

The literary critic then seeks to develop a coherent statement out of his initial response, the hypothesis which stimulated him to proceed with his investigation. The verbalization which this entails necessarily involves analysis of some kind, and this means that any unity the initial response may be supposed to have had disappears, along with its inchoateness, once it is broken down into aspectual features for the purpose of presentation through language. However highly subjective and impressionistic, however metaphorical, this presentation may be, it is inevitably discrete in form. Nevertheless, the critic has as his purpose, throughout his necessarily analytical treatment of the particular literary phenomena which are his concern, a presentation of his response which has not lost its unity. From the eighteenth century Jesuit theorists of the technique of *explication* to the literary critics of the present day, synthesis has been a major preoccupation of those concerned with the interpretation of literature.

This, of course, is to oversimplify. The very process of verbalization, and the discreteness of treatment which this requires, resolves itself into a dialectic. The critic's final statement is the result of continually glancing back at his immediate response, as it is checked against the text, with a concentration now upon one aspect, now upon another; upon its plot, its character presentation, its subject matter, its language, and upon the inter-relation of some or all of these. This is done in terms of the critic's general experience of literature, life, and language, and thus the text is never examined in complete isolation. So too, as the articulation of the critical statement proceeds, the response is constantly open to modification and development, and we are probably never presented with a statement which is simply derived from the immediate response.

Again, it is observable that only rarely in literary criticism is there anything approaching an equal concentration upon all aspects of the text. Sometimes it is the plot which dominates the critic's interest, sometimes character presentation or subject matter. The fundamental difficulty at this point is that different aspects of a work of literature are never completely separable, for it is by means of language that they are all realized and through language that they all impinge upon the critics' sensibility.

We are conscious of literary experiences which appear to transcend language: plot, character, personality, form in another sense . . . Yet all these experiences are communicated by linguistic means. This is the paradox with which we are confronted.[1]

This does not, however, mean that it is the language we are primarily concentrating on when we are examining these other aspects of the literary experience. Rather, we are dealing with aspectual abstractions. Here indeed we begin to confront the problem of style, and in order that a further increase in its multifarious definitions be avoided, we suggest that it may for the moment be resolved thus: when the language of a text is examined, not as a source of information about plot or character or thought, but as the major focus of attention in the dialectical process—that is when the response is primarily to the use of

1. R. A. Sayce, 'Literature and Language', *Essays in Criticism*, VII, 2.

language itself—the critic may be said to be examining the style of the text.

3

I t has for a long time been the literary critic's opinion that this is what he is doing when he concentrates on the use of language, and modern linguistics is in no position to deny him the use of the term 'stylistics'[1] to describe this aspect of literary study. If the linguist wishes to think of the study of style as merely the comparison of linguistic descriptions, he should, as M. A. K. Halliday does, qualify 'stylistics' with 'linguistic' and talk of linguistic stylistics.[2] There is certainly no doubt that linguistics today offers to the student of style tools of considerable precision for certain purposes; a precision which cannot be gainsaid whatever reservations may be felt about the claims of some linguists regarding the scientific nature of their theory and procedures.[3] In most schools of modern linguistics, however, the discipline is thought of as a

1. S. Ullmann has given a history of this 'ungainly term' in his *Style in the French Novel*, Cambridge 1957, p. 3, n. 2: 'The term *stilistik* has been in current use in German since the early nineteenth century; the first example recorded by Grimm's dictionary is from *Novalis*. In English the noun *stylistic* is found as early as 1846; *stylistics* is first attested in 1882–3 (O.E.D.). In French the first example of *stylistique* is from 1872, when Littré included the word in his dictionary.'

2. In 'The Linguistic Description of Literary Texts', a paper given at the Ninth International Congress of Linguists, 1962, and shortly to be published.

3. The view of some transformative-generative grammarians that linguistics should be a 'hard' science, whose theories and procedures must be open to 'strong' verification, is particularly to be regarded with suspicion. The predictive certainty they seek can be obtained only at the cost of neglecting the situational aspect of language, an aspect of prime importance in the study of style.

descriptive study of a part of human social behaviour, and as such, one which cannot share the predictive certainty and the techniques of controlled experiment open to the physical and biological sciences. Linguistics is, then, best thought of as a social science, and the linguist normally recognizes that he has more in common with the social anthropologist and the sociologist, both in his field of study and his techniques, than he has with the physicist or the biochemist.

It is in our decision to use descriptive linguistics as a component in the study of style, a component which aids in developing, modifying, and making more explicit our responses to the use of language in a text, it is in this that we diverge from, without rejecting or ignoring, the literary critic's traditional approach. The linguistic approach, involving as it does careful observation and detailed and consistent description of language phenomena, can be of great benefit in stylistic work, so long as it does not mean that one is asked to accept pseudo-procedural, statistically orientated definitions of style,[1] or to ignore the importance of response, including the impressionistic apprehension of linguistic features not amenable, at least at present, to description by the highly formal techniques of linguistics. For dealing with many aspects of imagery, for dealing with an author's deliberate restriction of a word's semantic field, or the eristic or evocative nature of many words in use, the theory of lexis,[2] for example, in so far as it has been formulated, is still of limited assistance.

On the other hand, linguistics does not simply provide theories and techniques; at its best it leads to the development and critical maintenance of a sensitive attitude to language. In the study of style one is as important as the other. This linguistic attitude is shared in some degree by most linguists. Nor is the literary critic without such an attitude. His may not be expressed in the same

1. See Enkvist, present volume, p. 25, and David Abercrombie, 'Pseudo-procedures in Linguistics,' *Zeitschrift für Phonetik, Sprachwissenschaft und Kommunikationsforschung*, Bd. 16, 1963, Heft 1–3.

2. See pp. 73–75.

terms as the linguist's, nor need he be expected to articulate a coherent account of it: this is not his central task. Nevertheless, an attitude to language that is both sensitive and possessed of an implicit internal coherence has always been a necessary part of the equipment, and a characteristic of, those concerned with the appreciative and interpretative study of literature. This will readily be granted by most linguists of such modern critics as T. S. Eliot, F. R. Leavis, and William Empson. But long before modern criticism emerged, with its emphasis on verbal analysis,[1] Sir Walter Raleigh, drawing upon his knowledge both of historical philology and of literature, demonstrated fine linguistic sophistication in his book *Style*.[2] The following passage is his robust rejection of the analogy between literature and architecture, an analogy which implies that words are the bricks of which literary edifices are built:

Finite and quite rigid words are not, in any sense that holds good of bricks. They move and change, they wax and wane, they wither and burgeon; from age to age, from place to place, from mouth to mouth, they are never at a stay. They take on colour, intensity and vivacity from the infection of neighbourhood; the same word is of several shapes and diverse imports in one and the same sentence. They depend on the building they compose for the very chemistry of the stuff that composes them. The same epithet is used in the phrases 'a fine day' and 'fine irony', in 'fair trade' and 'a fair goddess'. Were different symbols to be invented for these sundry meanings the art of literature would perish. For words carry with them all the meanings they have worn, and the writer shall be judged by those that he selects for prominence in the train of his thought. A slight technical implication, a faint tinge of archaism, in the common turn of speech that you employ, and in a moment you have shaken off the mob that scours the rutted highway, and are addressing a select audience of ticketholders within closed doors. A single natural phrase of peasant speech, a direct physical sense to a word that genteel parlance authorises readily enough in its metaphorical sense, and at a touch you have blown the roof off the drawing room of the villa, and have set its obscure inhabitants wriggling in the un-

1. The amount of verbal analysis in the critical work of F. R. Leavis has, however, been considerably exaggerated, as is recognized in George Watson, *The Literary Critics*, London, 1962, pp. 208–9.

2. London, 1918 (13th imp.), pp. 25–27.

accustomed sun. In choosing a sense for your words you choose also an audience for them.

Implicit in this passage is a recognition of some of the major premises of linguistics: the nature and importance of the addresser-addressee relationship, the inter-relationships between linguistic and non-linguistic contexts, the uniqueness of the phenomenon language, and the diachronic, diatopic and idiolectal dimensions of language differentiation.[1] One must admire also its elegant vigour, and its precisely evocative use of metaphor; a quality of writing rarely to be found in the work of modern linguists.

It might well be asked what, in the face of this, the linguist has to contribute. The value of his contribution should lie in the very explicitness and comprehensiveness of his statements about the language of a text or texts. This is what can, at the least, complement the perceptive yet often elusive statements of the literary critic.

4

IT is therefore necessary to ask in what specific respects a linguistic to be used for stylistic study should be comprehensive and explicit: what, in other words, does the student of style require of a linguistic description. What follows in this section cannot, of course, present a full account in all its details of any one linguistic —let alone deal adequately with the different contributions to stylistics made by various linguistic theories. Those readers acquainted with the field of language study will recognize that the point of view presented here derives very largely from the work

---

1. See Section 5.

in linguistics accomplished in Great Britain during the past two decades.[1] Our intention is, however, not so much to offer an account of a particular model, as to suggest what might be demanded of a linguistic model in stylistic study.

Language is transmitted either by audible sound-waves or by visible marks on a surface: that is, language substance is either phonic or graphic. A linguistic satisfactory for stylistic study needs, in the first place, to take account of this substantial aspect of language; and it needs also to possess the means of enabling us to recognize and deal adequately with the relationship between written and spoken language. Since graphic substance is related to, and in part derives from, phonic substance, all written language has some phonic potential. This leads, in turn, to the recognition, important, as we shall see, in stylistics, that much written language, particularly drama and poetry, is written with its phonic potential, the speaking of it, strongly in mind.

The formal aspect of language, that it exhibits patterns which are meaningful, has also to be acknowledged and dealt with adequately. The need for adequacy entails that the linguist be not only prepared to account formally for the grammar of a language —the type of contrastive word-order pattern which distinguishes in English 'dog bites man' from 'man bites dog'—but also with its phonology, which distinguishes, for example, 'she's a pretty girl' as statement from 'she's a pretty girl' as question, with its graphology, which distinguishes 'She's a pretty girl.' from 'She's a pretty girl?', and with its lexical form, which distinguishes 'she's an attractive girl' from 'she's a beautiful girl'. To suggest that these latter utterances differ because the meaning of 'attractive' is different from the meaning of 'beautiful' is linguistically and

---

1. This work is particularly associated with the names of the late J. R. Firth, and of A. McIntosh and M. A. K. Halliday. The present authors take full responsibility for what appears in this monograph, while at the same time wishing to express their indebtedness not only to the above linguists, but also to David Abercrombie, P. D. Strevens, S. Pit Corder, J. McH. Sinclair, and J. P. Thorne for private discussions on matters linguistic and stylistic.

descriptively to beg part of the question.[1] We know that the meaning differs, but the linguist will want to ask how far this difference can be accounted for in purely formal terms, without recourse to meaning in the explanation of meaning.

The linguistic must also help to give us an intelligent realization of the consequences of seeing language as part of human social behaviour. Language events do not take place in isolation from other events; rather they operate within a wider framework of human activity. Any piece of language is therefore part of a situation, and so has a context, a relationship with that situation. Indeed, it is this relationship between the substance and form of a piece of language on the one hand and the extra-linguistic circumstances in which it occurs on the other, which gives what is normally called 'meaning' to utterances.[2] At some stage or other, any linguistic description, if it is to be complete, must take this relationship into consideration.

1. Cf. M. A. K. Halliday, 'Categories of the Theory of Grammar', *Word*, 17, iii, 1961, pp. 244–5; 'Language has "formal meaning" and "contextual meaning" . . . The formal meaning of an item is its operation in the network of formal relations. Contextual meaning, which is an extension of the popular—and traditional linguistic—notion of meaning, is quite distinct from formal meaning . . .'

2. This relationship for Halliday is the 'interlevel' of *context*, and he points out ('Categories', p. 245) that 'The contextual meaning of an item is its relation to extra-textual features; but this is not a direct relation to the item as such, but of the item in its place in linguistic form: contextual meaning is therefore logically dependent on formal meaning.' Also 'the reason why "context" is preferred to "semantics" as the name of this interlevel is that "semantics" is too closely tied to one particular method of statement, the conceptual method . . . The latter, by attempting to link language form to unobservables, becomes circular, since concepts are only observable as (exponents of) the forms they are set up to "explain". The linguistic statement of context attempts to relate language form to (abstractions from) other (i.e. extratextual) observables.' What we regard as an inadequacy in much American linguistics (both transformative-generative and structural) arises from the failure to give due emphasis to this aspect of language study. British linguists have not solved the many problems it raises but these problems are at least recognized as being of concern to the linguist.

Stylistic studies are primarily concerned with the examination of written language. It might be thought therefore that phonology has little to contribute. However, as has been already suggested, certain kinds of literature have strong phonic potential. Drama and much verse are written with the spoken word in mind, and particular linguistic features which they consequently exhibit cannot be fully accounted for without a reasonably sophisticated phonology. This phonology should be able to help throw light on such features as alliteration, assonance, rhyme, pararhyme, onomatopoeia, rhythm, and metre. Classical prosody as traditionally applied to English verse could well be modified in the light of phonological studies of this nature.[1]

Thus, for example, the phonemic recurrences characteristic of Hopkins' alliteration cannot be fully understood or described simply in terms of the repetition of initial sounds, which is the definition of this device commonly provided by works on prosody and poetics. The complexity of Hopkins' alliteration, and indeed that of many other poets, requires a recognition of the manner in which vowel contrasts and transitions, consonantal groupings according to the place and manner of their articulation, consonant clusters and positional shifts of the same phonemic units in the structure of succeeding syllables, are all counterpointed, so to speak, to provide a total effect. These are often linked to stress patterns, which are themselves part of larger patternings, of which the metrical line is one.

This suggests that a satisfactory phonology would postulate units to cope with a whole range of contrasts of differing status carried by stretches of sound of different lengths: contrasts in the structure of syllables, contrasts of stress, and of intonation pattern. Any or all of this range of contrasts may be of particular significance in any text, spoken or written, and we need categories to describe them. Also required, for purposes of descriptive con-

1. David Abercrombie's 'Syllable Quantity and Enclitics in English', *In Honour of Daniel Jones*, London, 1964, and 'A Phonetician's View of Verse Structure', *Linguistics*, 6, 1964, have much to offer here.

sistency and power, is that the various units be viewed in hierarchical relation to each other.[1]

But the fact remains that when studying style we are usually faced with written texts, graphic substance. It is also evident that a precise statement of the relationships between the patterns of phonic substance and those of graphic substance is not easy, particularly in a language such as English. There is certainly no one-to-one correspondence. Nevertheless, it is clear that the graphic substance of English does exhibit patterns: English spelling is not random—for one thing, not all possible combinations of letters can occur. Like English phonology it is polysystemic, even if its systems, in part the result of long historical processes, are notably complicated. Writing has its own means, however inadequate they may be, of indicating some of the patterned contrasts discernible in spoken language. One might instance written language's use of the alphabet, and of combinations of some of its letters, to represent certain, but not all, of the sounds of the language user; its use of punctuation, italicization, capitalization, and so on, to deal, in some measure, with features such as stress and intonation. Written language may also have systems for indicating contrasts which are unconnected with the phonological contrasts of the spoken medium, but as yet there is no clear and satisfactory statement of them. Graphology, the patterned systems of the graphic substance of language and their study presents a field of investigation in which much is yet to be done, work which might prove to be of relevance to the stylistic study of written texts. Our linguistic must be open to such developments.

Phonological, and in a different way, graphological patterns

1. See M. A. K. Halliday, 'The Tones of English', *Archivum Linguisticum*, XV, i. The units postulated for English are *tone group*, the unit of contrastive intonation contour, *foot*, the unit of contrastive stress, *syllable*, the unit of contrastive syllabic structure, and *phonematic unit*, or *phoneme*, the unit of contrastive articulation. They are thought of as arranged in a hierarchy or 'rank scale', descending from the *tone group* to the *phoneme*, each unit consisting of one or more of the units immediately below it in the hierarchy.

may be seen as the framework of regularity and contrast which link language substance with language form. Certain aspects of the phonology of a language are given, as it were; the individual speaker of English cannot start, of his own accord, successfully making an aspirated 'p' sound contrast meaningfully with an unaspirated 'p'. Phonology is therefore often thought of as that which relates the substance of a language to its form, as an 'interlevel'.[1] Because it derives its patterns from phonology, graphology is thought of as relating graphic substance to form by way of phonology. It must still, however, be recognized that certain aspects of phonology provide the user of a language with the means of making a meaningful choice, the sort of choice normally accounted for by grammar. In spoken language the choice of a certain intonation pattern rather than another makes an utterance which is, in other respects, grammatically a statement into a question, as does the graphological choice of the query mark rather than the period mark in written language. In other words phonology and graphology not only connect substance to form, they are themselves aspects of form, patterns which on occasions directly make substance meaningful in a situation.

The study of linguistic form is the examination of the way languages carry contrast in meaning through their internal structure. The linguistic description of the form of any particular language is, then, the description of the meaningful internal patterns of that language, the isolation of those places in the language where there are possibilities of choice which contribute to meaning. What is to be asked of a linguistic in this respect, is whether it helps the analyst in recognizing and accounting for all the places in the language where there is a possibility of such choices, and whether it helps him with the task of stating the range of possible choices at each such place. In this respect the value of a sound and sufficiently complex phonology and graphology has

1. See M. A. K. Halliday, 'Categories', p. 244, and the discussion of 'level' and 'interlevel' in Robert M. W. Dixon, *Linguistic Science and Logic*, The Hague, 1963, pp. 21–29.

already been indicated. It is, however, grammar (morphology and syntax) which has dominated the description of form, which has in recent years been most refined in linguistics,[1] and which promises most for the analysis of style. Nevertheless, the observable fact that the extent of the range of possible choices varies at different places in a language, that at some only a few choices are open, and at others many, is what led us to suggest earlier that a linguistic capable of providing the sort of formal description most useful for stylistic study does well to draw a distinction within form such as that made by certain linguists in Britain between grammar and lexis. Grammar deals with all those places where there is a choice that has to be made between a small and limited number of possibilities. In other words grammar can deal descriptively where the choice is between, say, a passive or active verbal group, between a positive or negative verbal group, between a singular or plural nominal group, between a declarative or interrogative clause, and so on.[2] So grammar can indicate where and why 'sit' differs from 'be seated', 'to be' from 'not to be', ' man of Harlech' from 'men of Harlech', 'It was done.' from 'Was it done?'. A really useful grammar can also distinguish formally 'the book which is lying on the table is mine' from 'the book lying on the table is mine', and both of these from 'the book on the table is mine', at the same time as it shows the measure of their structural similarity. But grammar cannot indicate why 'he

1. See e.g. C. C. Fries, *The Structure of English*, New York, 1952; M. A. K. Halliday, 'Grammatical Categories in Modern Chinese', *Transactions of the Philological Society*, 1956; M. Chomsky, *Syntactic Structures*, The Hague, 1957; A. A. Hill, *Introduction to Linguistic Structures*, New York, 1958; E. Nida, *Synopsis of English Syntax*, Norman, Oklahoma, 1960; M. A. K. Halliday, 'Categories', 1961.

2. Such choices are choices within a closed system. Closed systems are characteristic of grammar. Choices which do not operate within closed systems, 'open' choices, are characteristic of lexis. See M. A. K. Halliday, 'Linguistique Genérale et Linguistique Appliquée à l'Enseignement des Langues', *Publications du Centre de Linguistique Appliquée* Université de Besançon, 1962, pp. 8–9 and 20–22. Also 'Categories', pp. 263–8.

had a fear' differs from 'he had a hope'. A very delicate grammar can volunteer the information that 'fear' and 'hope' belong to the same sub-class of nouns, but it cannot distinguish 'fear' from 'hope'; at least no grammar has yet done so. Indeed it has often been thought that such a distinction is outside the scope of formal description, and that semantics takes over where grammar ends. But there is no necessity for formal description to end with grammar.

Theoretical categories are required for the formal description of lexis, and two fundamental ones, *collocation* and *set* have been proposed.[1] Collocation is set up to account for the tendency of certain items in a language to occur close to each other, a tendency not completely explained by grammar. For example, the item 'economy' is likely to occur in the same linguistic environment as items such as 'affairs', 'policy', 'plan', 'programme', 'disaster'— most of us could compile quite a long list. These items are termed the *collocates* of 'economy' which, because it is the item under examination, is itself termed the *nodal item*.[2] A list of collocates of the nodal item constitute its collocational range. In formal lexical study, of course, the establishment of the collocational range of an item would be the result of a statistical investigation covering a wide range of texts. If 'finance' were taken as the nodal item, and a collocational range established for it, it would probably emerge that there was a considerable overlap with the range of 'economy', that these two items share a significant number of collocates. So too, perhaps, if one took 'industry' as the nodal item. These three items could then be grouped together into a *set*, the second theoretical category of lexis, which accounts for the tendency of items to share part of their collocational range, to have a collocational overlap.

1. See M. A. K. Halliday, 'Categories', pp. 273–7. The many problems, theoretical and procedural, still to be faced in the formal study of lexis are clearly outlined in J. McH. Sinclair, 'Beginning the Study of Lexis', to appear in a volume of studies in commemoration of J. R. Firth.

2. See J. C. Catford, *A Linguistic Theory of Translation*, London, 1965.

It will be clear that what constitutes a set in any description depends upon both the nature and the amount of data being examined, and upon the delicacy of the description; that is, its degree of detail and specificity. The linguist may group together as a set items having only a small mutual collocational range. On the other hand he may demand that they have a good deal of their collocational range in common before he so groups them. He may even demand that they share collocations at a number of removes from themselves, at a distance of one, two or three or more lexical items. The more mutual collocational range demanded as the criterion for a set, the smaller the sets and the more delicate the description. Lexical sets, then, are 'open' as compared with the 'closed' nature of grammatical systems.

It may be asked what are the advantages of this formal handling of lexis. Items such as 'economy', 'finance', and 'industry' could, after all, be grouped together on purely semantic grounds. However, when compared to the referential criterion of meaning, the formal criterion of collocation has this in its favour: it is more observational and objective. Its disadvantage for the analyst of style is that it demands large-scale frequency counts, the extensive statistical examination of many texts. Such work is only just beginning, and so in the study of style semantically rather than collocationally determined sets have often to be established. Nevertheless an awareness of current work by linguists on the theory of lexis is already valuable in that it throws light on certain aspects of 'chain' (one thing *after* another) and 'choice' (one thing *rather* than another) relationships in language not revealed either by grammar or traditional lexicography.

Collocation is an important concept to have in mind when studying the language of literature. This is because the creative writer often achieves some of his effects through the interaction between usual and unusual collocations, and through the creation of new, and therefore stylistically significant, collocations. This is particularly noticeable in poetry. In Dylan Thomas's 'In the room / So loud to my own', one's response to these lines is the result of an awareness of the usual set of items which would be likely to occur between 'the room so . . .' and '. . . to my own', a set producing collocations such as 'so *close* to my own' and 'so *near* to my own'. We contrast these with the normal collocations of 'loud' and realize that it has been led as it were, to share here two ranges of collocation. This is important in an examination of how we respond to the use of language in this poem, 'Vision and Prayer', where we also encounter such collocational shifts as 'the *heart*print of man' and 'the inmost marrow of my *heart* bone'. And indeed, Dylan Thomas's verse abounds in collocations of this kind: 'a *grief* ago', 'once *below* a time', 'happy as the *heart* was long', 'all the *sun* long', 'it was Adam and *maiden*'. The concepts of collocation and set are therefore indispensable in the study of metaphor.

All this is not to minimize the value, in the study of style, of such great works of lexicographic scholarship as the *Oxford English Dictionary* and *Webster's Third International Dictionary*. They make available a great range of organized linguistic information: orthographic, phonetic, grammatical, historical and comparative, and contextual (provided by the definitions). The formal description of lexis to be found in them is, however, limited. It is provided by the citations, examples of a particular word in use with other words. This gives an indication of its collocations, a glimpse of the lexical company it keeps and no more. A thesaurus, in which the sets are collocationally determined, is needed as a complement to the dictionary. It would also be a complement, in formal description, to the grammars of the language. 'Fear' and 'hope', 'beautiful' and 'attractive', these pairs may be beyond grammatical distinction, but they may well be distinguished lexically according to their different collocational ranges and their membership of different sets.

The formal relationships observable in language require above all, however, a sophisticated grammar. Fortunately, over the last few decades, as was noted, linguistic science has shifted its attention from phonemic and morphemic analysis to grammar, and

75

very interesting work has been and is being done in America, by linguists both of the structuralist and transformative-generative schools, such as A. A. Hill and S. R. Levin, on the application of different types of grammatical analysis to stylistic study.[1] In Britain development in the field of grammar has led particularly to the realization that it is necessary in grammar, as in linguistic description generally, to distinguish between, and have an articulated idea of, the relationship between theoretical and descriptive categories. It has been realized that in the 'linguistic study of language', as in other scientific activities, the more complex and explicit the theory, the simpler and more coherent the description. It is thought necessary, therefore, that a general theory of grammar should lie behind the grammatical description of any particular language, and that the categories which are set up for the purpose of such description should derive from theoretical categories. The contribution which this view of grammatical description may make to stylistics must now be considered.

M. A. K. Halliday has postulated four theoretical categories of grammar.[2] These are *unit*, *structure*, *class*, and *system*, and they are intended to account for the fundamental grammatical patterns of all languages, in that workable descriptive categories may be derived from them. They themselves derive not only from the examination of particular languages but, perhaps more importantly, from the contemplation of language as an activity. In this activity one item follows another as though in a chain, and the language user chooses one item rather than another at places along that chain, and it is because of these essential characteristics of language that the four categories can be postulated and regarded as general. The category of unit, which accounts for those

---

1. E.g. A. A. Hill, 'Towards a Literary Analysis', *Univ. of Virginia Studies*, 4, 1951, 'An Analysis of the "Windhover": an experiment in structural method', *Publications of the Modern Language Association of America*, 70, 1955, and 'A Program for the Definition of Literature', *Univ. of Texas Studies of English*, 37, 1958; S. R. Levin, *Linguistic Structures in Poetry*, The Hague, 1962.

2. 'Categories'.

stretches of language of varying extent which carry, recurrently, meaningful patterns, and the category of structure, which is concerned with the nature of these patterns themselves, are both primarily derived from and intended to account for the chain aspect of language. On the other hand the category of class, which arranges items in the language according to the way they operate in patterns, and the category of system, which accounts for those limited groups of possibilities from which choices must be made at certain places in the patterns, are both primarily derived from and intended to account for the choice aspect of language. These grammatical categories are clearly at a higher level of abstraction than those which more traditional grammar has made familiar. Hence their more general applicability to languages.

The more familiar categories, like singular and plural, noun and verb, subject and complement, clause and sentence, are descriptive categories, instances in the description of a particular language, such as English, of the theoretical categories: sentence and clause are instances of unit; subject and complement are names for certain elements in the patterns or structures which make up the clause; noun and verb are examples of word classes; singular and plural are mutually exclusive possibilities of choice in a system. Such categories or terms, originally derived from Greek and Latin grammarians, are not universally applicable— they wou'd not, for example, all be useful in the description of many non-Indo-European languages. A realization that they are not general categories of grammar has led linguists in Britain to re-define and modify them, in terms of what is a general theory of grammar, before using them in the description of English.[1]

Notions of unit, structure, class, and system did, of course, lie beh'nd much of what is often called traditional grammar. Nevertheless a more overt and reflective awareness of them is leading to

1. Several grammars which are likely to have remarkably fewer 'exceptions' in their descriptions of English than those derived from a largely latinate grammar are expected to appear in the next few years.

greater rigour and consistency in their application to the description of particular languages. This is largely because of the delineation by Halliday of three scales of abstraction which link the categories to each other and to the language data.[1] An explanation of these three scales, of *rank*, *delicacy*, and *exponence*, will, the present authors believe, throw most light on how this type of grammar, sometimes known as *category-scale* grammar, may help to contribute to the description and analysis of style.

The scale of rank is the hierarchical ordering of the units recognized in the description of a particular language. In English five units are at present recognized: sentence, clause, group, word, and morpheme. They are thought of as arranged in a hierarchy or rank-scale, descending from the most inclusive (the sentence) to the least inclusive (the morpheme). This means that a sentence consists of one or more clauses, a clause of one or more groups, a group of one or more words, and a word of one or more morphemes. Morpheme is the smallest unit recognized in the grammar of the language, and so has itself no grammatical structure. Thus, Othello's cry of 'Devil!' (IV, i, 236) is a sentence, which consists of one clause, which consists of one group, itself consisting of one word, which in turn consists of one morpheme. Normally, clauses make up, or operate in, the structure of the sentence, groups operate in the structure of the clause, words operate in the structure of the group, and morphemes operate in the structure of words. So in the clause 'Queen Elizabeth has been our monarch for many years of peace', the group 'Queen Elizabeth' is the subject (S) of the clause, the group 'has been' is the predicator (P), the group 'our monarch' is the complement (C), and the group 'for many years of peace' is the adjunct(A).[2]

---

1. 'Categories', pp. 268–73. The concept of 'delicacy' was originated by A. McIntosh.

2. Classes of a unit may be set up according to the criterion of potentiality of operation in the structure of the unit next above it in rank. So groups may be classed according to how they operate in clause structure. Those groups which can operate at S, C and in some cases also at A (such as 'this very

In the group 'our monarch' the word 'our' is the modifier (M) to the head word (H) 'monarch'. So too, in 'for many years of peace', the word 'for' is the binder (B) introducing the group, the word 'many' is the modifier to the head word 'years'. However, the post-modifier or qualifier (Q) to that head is in this case not itself a word but a group, with the structure B ('of') H ('peace').

Indeed it is a feature of all language that a unit sometimes operates in the structure of a unit of the same or of lower rank. Thus, in Sir Thomas Browne's 'How shall the dead arise, is no question of my Faith', the clause 'How shall the dead arise' (itself with the structure APSP) is the subject of the clause 'How shall the dead arise (S), is (P) no question of my Faith (C)'. And in the Prayer Book's 'We have done those things we ought not to have done' the clause 'we (S) ought not to have done (P)' is operating as qualifier to the head 'things' in the nominal group 'those things we ought not to have done' (structure MHQ), which is itself the complement to the predicator 'have done' in the clause 'We (S) have done (P) those things we ought not to have done (C)'. And if we were to add to this clause 'knowing thy love', we would have 'We have done those things we ought not to have done knowing thy love', and 'knowing thy love' would be a non-finite clause[1] (structure PC) at adjunct in a clause, itself the qualifier in a nominal group at complement in another clause. To account for this type of phenomenon the concept of rank-shift is postulated. A clause operating not directly in the structure of a sentence but in the structure of another clause, as subject or complement (traditionally termed noun clauses) or as adjunct (including both the traditional adverbial and non-

---

year') are *nominal* groups; those which operate at P only (such as 'has passed') are *verbal* groups; and those which operate only at A (such as 'very quickly') are *adverbial* groups.

1. There seems little point in perpetuating the idea that it is useful to recognize as a clause in English only those which contain a finite verb. Many clauses are subjectless: one has only to think of such common utterances as 'Sit down!', 'Come here!', 'Go away!', 'Why do it?', 'Coming?' and 'Coming!'.

defining relative clauses) can be thought of as first-stage rank-shift clauses. Those clauses operating in the structure of a group (say at Q)—traditionally defining relative clauses—may be termed second-stage rank-shift clauses. Defining and non-defining relative clauses, frequently distinguished notionally, can thus be distinguished formally according to the different rank of unit in the structure of which they are operating. Occasionally, usually in idiom expressions, a clause operates in the structure of a word, as in *'ne'er do wells'*. This is a third-stage rank-shift clause. The only non-rank-shift clauses in English, then, are those commonly known as main clauses. So we see that sentence structure is either simple, (one non-rank-shifted clause) or compound (more than one such clause). Complexity begins at the rank of the clause.[1]

The scale of rank and the concept of rank-shift make clear and help to describe accurately the infrastructuring nature of language: how a number of units act as one in the structure of another unit; how structure in language is not a mere linear progression, but has depth also. They help to isolate and illuminate where the structural complexity in a text lies. In the description of the style of an individual text, and in the comparison of the styles of more than one text, the value of this will be apparent. Together with the scale of delicacy they help to discover where the structural similarities and where the structural dissimilarities between texts are locatable in their language.

Delicacy 'is the scale of differentiation or depth in detail'. When a description is at its least delicate, it will set up only the least number of units, classes, elements of structure or systems which the data makes necessary. If any structural analysis is to be made of the verbal group in English, three elements have to be assigned to it: H (head), M (modifier, that which may precede the head) and Q (qualifier, that which may succeed the head). This would make possible the least delicate description.

1. This view of the structure of the English sentence is at variance with that held at present by M. A. K. Halliday (personal communication).

At this degree of delicacy, the two verbal groups

> was/beaten/up
> may have been being/beaten/up

have the same structure MHQ. A more delicate description of the verbal group would, however, recognize further structure within the element M — m (modal modifier) pe (perfective aspect modifier) c (continuous aspect modifier) pa (passive voice modifier). If we now analyse these two verbal groups we can assign to them the structures M(pa)HQ and M(m pe c pa)HQ. (pa) and (m pe c pa) are more delicate statements of structure and have helped us not only to differentiate between the two verbal groups, but to show where the differences lie at the same time as the structural analysis at its least delicate shows their measure of similarity.

The scale of exponence or exemplification relates the categories of the theory, which are categories of the highest degree of abstraction, to the data. For example, one might say 'the exponent of the subject element of structure in the clause "kinde pitty chokes my spleene" is a nominal group with the structure MH. The exponent of M is a prenominal word, and of H a nominal word. The exponent of the prenominal word is "kinde" and the exponent of the nominal word is "pitty".' The relationship between the scale of exponence and rank will be clear in this example, how the exponent of an element of structure at one rank is likely to be a unit of the rank below; but exponence is a distinct scale because at any one rank we can give a concrete exemplification and could have said, for instance, that 'kinde pitty' is the exponent of S in the clause structure. This, however, as Halliday neatly remarks when discussing the relationship of exponence and rank, would be 'not a description of the element S, since by relating it to its exponents at a stage when it was not necessary to do so we should have lost generality. So instead of throwing up the grammatical sponge and moving out to lexis while this is still avoidable, the description takes successive steps down the exponence scale, changing rank where necessary, until (at the degree of delicacy chosen) it is brought unavoidably face to face with the formal item.'[1]

Formal items are meaningful stretches of language of any extent. They may be divided into grammatical items and lexical items. Grammatical items (such as the 's' of 'loves' in 'he loves') are fully explicable in grammar. Lexical items (such as 'pound') are not fully explicable in grammar and enter into collocations and open set choices. So lexis takes over where the most delicate grammar ends. 'Pound' is the graphological exponent of at least four different lexical items; one which collocates with such items as 'stone', 'ounce', 'weight', another which collocates with items such as 'shilling', 'pence', 'sterling', another which collocates with 'sheep', 'cattle', 'village', etc., and yet another which collocates with 'pestle', 'mortar', and 'yam'.

The scale of exponence, then, keeps the describer of language constantly aware of his data, and where he is in relation to his data. This is important, for one of the ways in which linguistics differs from other branches of scholarship which study language, is that it studies it in its own terms. This means that it insists on formal criteria, and avoids, wherever possible, extra-linguistic criteria and notional definitions. In other words, definitions, explanations and so on are derived from language and the data of language, and expressed in terms of it, and of abstractions from that data. This does not mean that the linguist is not concerned with meaning. He must often use his appreciation of meaning to discover what he has to describe formally; and the very purpose of his work is to throw light on different aspects of linguistic meaning. But his insistence on formal criteria is what gives his statements about meaning in language, as opposed to the philosopher's, the psychologist's or the literary critic's, their own particular and peculiar value.

More emphasis has been placed, in recent years, on the linguistic description of contemporary language than on historical

1. 'Categories', p. 271.

linguistics. The student of style cannot afford, however, to neglect the historical study of language, particularly as many of his texts will lie outside the modern period. Questions about differences in phonology (did the final '-ed' have syllabic quantity at this time?), in graphology (was the punctuation of this time or this author meant to be 'logical', 'grammatical', or 'rhetorical'?), in grammar (was there a 'you/thee *or* thou' system operating at this time?) or in lexis (were the collocations of 'wanton' significantly different then from now?), must often be in the stylistic analyst's mind when he is examining a non-contemporary text. And modern linguistics could help him if more attention was given to the problem of describing languages comprehensively and systematically at different stages in their history.

Linguistic science has a history stretching over many centuries. It has had its dark ages and its renaissances, and it has still much to do; but it does now offer a body of scholarship concerning language which the student of literature can ill afford to ignore.

5

A RECOGNITION of the dual and complementary value of intuitive judgement of language use on the one hand, and the more objective techniques of description of language phenomena which modern linguistics makes available on the other, is necessary and indeed fundamental to this view of stylistic study. Our suggestion is that these two approaches to language, the one characteristic of literary criticism and the other of linguistic analysis—and both involving sensitivity to language if the literary critic is to be more than a hack and the linguist more than a technician—can be brought together for stylistic investigation into a relationship which goes beyond the merely complementary.

This type of investigation, the close study of a text for the purposes of examining its style, involves, as was suggested in Section 3, the development of a considered response to the use of language in it; implying, in Jakobson's terms, a concentration upon the '"set" towards the message'.[1] If impressionistic reactions to the language of the text are to be more than complemented, if they are rather to be developed and modified by the application to them of the categories of linguistics, and if the final developed response is to be made explicit, the stages in this dialectical process need to be clear. This is not to suggest that procedures must be allowed to dominate the process. Procedural rigidity can too easily destroy initiative and intuitive power, with a consequent loss of sensitivity and flexibility. But consciousness of a 'procedural model' should be present in the mind of the student of style, whatever short cuts or adaptations he may need to use in any particular investigation.

If a mature literary-linguistic intuition provides clues, indicating certain linguistic features as likely to be of prime importance in establishing a text's particular style, the function of linguistic description is not simply that of making the precise nature of these features explicit, or of producing statistical tables to support the intuitive judgement. Such a procedure involves the danger of fixing the significant stylistic features in advance of careful analysis, thereby closing the door against the possibility of modifying and developing the original 'hypothesis'. It can also result in too ready a reliance upon impressionistically conceived and generalized norms of style, with a consequent failure to observe the essential distinction between shared and unique features in the language of a text; to a conflation, that is, of features characteristic of a period or a group with the idiosyncratic features of the individual writer, or of either of these with the specific use of language in a particular text. It may well be, as Kroeber suggests, that 'judgment and recognition of style are primary,

1. Roman Jakobson, 'Closing Statement: Linguistics and Poetics', *Style in Language*, ed. T. A. Sebeok, Technology Press and Wiley, 1960, p. 356.

analysis and statistics secondary'.[1] But it is necessary to emphasize that a rigorous checking, by means of a description of the total complex of features possessed by the text, of features intuitively judged to be stylistically significant, is likely to uncover other, previously unobserved, significant features; or to demonstrate the interrelationship of a series of features in such a way as to offer new, or at least modified, responses to the text as a whole. In this way our responses to the style of a text are open to progressive development. Only if we refuse to recognize the validity of responses which result from careful textual study, only if we believe that the immediate, spontaneous response to a work of literature is the sole criterion for critical statements, can such development be regarded with suspicion.

But before impressions are tested and developed in this way it is necessary to interpose a step of considerable importance, which may be termed the *placing of the text*. Failure to undertake some procedure of this sort has often led to error or distorted judgement. Placing the text may be seen as an attempt to objectivize the position of the language of the text in relation to the total available range of language, by reference to *institutional* categories, or dimensions, of usage.

It will be clear that one essential dimension required for placing a text must be historical. The language range of any period can be seen as one of the factors which both restrains the writer's linguistic choices and offers him certain creative opportunities. Linguistic restraints and opportunities, grammatical, lexical, phonological, and even graphological, are never precisely the same in one period as in another. The possibilities for grammatical innovation which the English of Shakespeare's time offered to the creative writer were not the same as those offered by the English of the Augustan period, for example. If all language is perpetually in a state of slow change, which continuously affects it at every level, it must follow that the writer's opportunities of choice, both

1. From *Style and Civilisation*, Ithaca, 1957, quoted by Dell H. Hymes, 'Phonological Aspects of Style: some English sonnets', Sebeok, *op. cit.*, p. 114.

conventional and creative (the possibilities, in transformationalist terms, for rule-governed and rule-forming creativity), must also change over time.

In relation to the language of the past the literary artist is in a special position. The language of poetry, in particular, has rarely been confined as strictly as other literary forms within the usage range of the language of its period. Poetry, and to a more restricted degree other literary genres, is able to draw upon some of the linguistic patterns of past periods. In placing a text historically, therefore, the student of style needs to be conscious of this historical range in the language available to the writer.

The second dimension to be applied in the placing of texts is that which defines their dialectal range. In any period the linguistic opportunities open to a writer will be determined by his chosen dialect. The advent of a standard form of the language for writing has, of course, affected this situation, to the extent of reducing the degree of difference in this respect we are likely to encounter among texts of the same period. Apart from synthetic poetic dialects like Lallans, therefore, we are unlikely to be faced in contemporary literature with dialectal differences as great as those, for example, which mark off the language of Chaucer from that of his contemporary the Gawain poet. Nevertheless, even today, it would be unwise to overlook the linguistic differences which arise from dialectal variation between the novels, for example, of Sillitoe and Salinger. And within a single work of literature, especially in the case of a play or a novel, dialectal shifts may be used for a variety of purposes.

Three additional inter-related dimensions which provide a valuable means of defining distinctions of linguistic usage not accounted for by reference to historical or dialectal differences, are those for which the present authors use the terms *field* of discourse, *mode* of discourse and *tenor* of discourse.[1]

---

1. The three categories have been variously defined, and named, by British linguists in the past few years. Sometimes, though in the view of the present authors not very helpfully, they have been subsumed under a major category

The field of discourse of a text relates to its subject-matter, and the linguistic features which may be associated with it. It is obvious that in non-literary texts of certain kinds the field of discourse will exercise marked influences upon the grammar and, in particular, upon the lexis, especially if the field is of a technical or specialized nature. Since the literary artist is free to draw upon all possible fields of discourse, and in certain instances may wish to utilize the linguistic resources of certain specialized fields for dramatic, poetic or evocative purposes, this dimension may need to be applied in examining the language of literature. In long texts there may be shifts in the field of discourse, and these will have linguistic consequences.

The mode of discourse is the dimension which accounts for the linguistic differences which result from the distinction between spoken and written discourse. All written language may be spoken, but it is noticeable that spoken language as such displays many features not present in written language, differences which cannot be accounted for simply by the differences between graphic and phonic substance, but which are also grammatical and lexical. These may be said to result from the differences between the situations in which written and spoken language tend to operate and the conventions associated with them. The literary artist may wish what he writes to be read as if it is spoken,

---

of *register*: e.g. McIntosh, Halliday, and Strevens, *The Linguistic Sciences and Language Teaching*, London, 1964, 'Registers may be distinguished according to field of discourse, mode of discourse, and style of discourse'. For obvious reasons we prefer *tenor* to *style* in this context. In J. C. Catford, *op. cit.*, the terms *mode* and *style* are used as above, but the term *register* corresponds approximately to that of *field*. Barbara Strang, *Modern English Structure*, London, 1962, uses the term *medium* in place of *mode*, and uses *style* and *register* in slightly different senses from any of the above. Terminology and definition in this area of language study are both clearly in a developing stage; and the part played by *genre* and a consciousness of *genre* in language choices has still to be stated and reconciled with these other dimensions of language variation. *Genre* can certainly be seen from one point of view as the conventional framework which preserves for use by the contemporary writer older forms of the language, forms no longer in extra-literary use.

in order to give the illusion of speech; or to be read as if it is over-heard, to give the impression of a spoken monologue. Or, if he is a dramatist, he will write in the expectation, or at least the hope, that what he writes will be presented orally. And the poet too will be very conscious of certain features of the spoken mode.

This is not to suggest that in any of these cases the language presented will have precisely the features which mark spontane-ous spoken language. It will usually be sufficiently marked to provide an illusion of speech; or, in the case of poetry, certain effects possible in spoken language, particularly phonological effects, are likely to determine, in part, the organization of the language.

Characters in plays and novels never talk quite like people do in life; were they to do so they would be intolerable. But it is important to discover which linguistic markers of mode the writer is using to provide his illusion. In novels he can, if he wishes, simply use graphological means, such as the use of quotation marks and occasional contracted forms, to mark the dialogue off from the narrative. On the other hand he may choose to use a wide range of features, graphological, lexical, and grammatical, for this purpose. The degree to which there are such shifts of mode within one work will depend on the writer's purposes and aims. One may compare in this respect the dialogue in Ivy Compton-Burnett's novels with that in Henry Green's; or the speeches of Ben Johnson's characters with those of Beaumont and Fletcher's; or, in poetry, and within one work, the shifts of mode which T. S. Eliot uses with such advantage in *The Waste Land*. Under-standing the ranges of language associated with differing modes offers the opportunity of relating the language of a text to the author's purposes and the effects he is aiming at.

The tenor of discourse is concerned with the degree of formality in the situation which the language mirrors, which can be said generally to depend upon the relationship between the speaker (or writer) and hearer (or reader). This dimension must be seen as a continuum, with no points between the two poles of extreme formality and extreme informality capable of being defined with any precision. Yet, as every native user of a language is aware, different places on this scale are marked by linguistic differences. Shifts of tenor may be used in literature, and not only in dialogue, to produce certain effects.

A poet or a novelist having chosen to use a particular tenor, for the purpose of defining his intended relationship with his reader, certain linguistic consequences will follow; or, more accurately, the tenor of the discourse will be determined for the reader by certain features in the language the writer uses. First-person narrative in the novel often tends to incline the language further along the scale towards the informal than does third person narrative. A number of contemporary novelists, such as Kerouac, Salinger, Barstow, and Sillitoe, are experimenting with forms of narrative, usually in the first person, which are much more informal in tenor than those which would have been used by their predecessors. This informality of tenor is the product of their language.

Shifts of tenor in dialogue are, of course, often used to reflect shifts in relationships between characters in the drama and the novel; since tenor of discourse is situation-tied, the linguistic markers characteristic of particular points on the tenor scale can be used to evoke situations and define relationships.

The dimensions of field, mode and tenor of discourse are, as has been suggested, inter-related and inter-acting. Certain fields of discourse are associated more with one mode than another; a shift of mode is often accompanied by a shift in tenor, and vice versa. Provided this inter-relationship is borne in mind, however, these dimensions of differentiation can usefully be applied, wherever appropriate, together with the historical and dialectal dimensions, in the task of placing the text, or parts of it, and of checking impressionistic judgements of language norms against describable linguistic features. This is a safeguard against overlooking certain effects which derive from the language of the text, or of misinterpreting them even where we are conscious of them. If the writer's range is potentially the whole of the language, we shall by this means see more clearly from which 'areas' of the language he is electing to make his choices in any particular instance.

The procedure of placing the text by reference to informed impressionistic norms defined in relation to period, dialect, field, mode and tenor of discourse, and their checking in terms of specific linguistic markers, where necessary comparing the text with other texts recognized to be of a similar type, provides a means of bringing shared and unique features into contrastive relief. Consequently, the danger of overemphasizing the idiosyncratic element in the use of language is reduced, and, in addition, a corrective is provided against overpersonalized interpretations of stylistic features. This procedure also permits the contrasts between shared and unique features to become part of the total dialectical process of arriving at a considered and explicit response to the style of a text.

By the time that a careful scrutiny of the text in such terms has been undertaken it is likely not only that the original response will be developing, but also that certain patterns of features will have suggested themselves as being worth investigating for the light which a description of them can throw upon certain intrinsic characteristics of the style. The focus is therefore now shifted from setting features in the text against norms of usage to viewing the patterns of choice within the text from the standpoint of their uniqueness. A selective description must therefore follow of those features chosen for investigation in these terms. It must be borne in mind that these features will form a complex, that examination of them in detail may well lead to the need to investigate other related features, and that lexis, grammar, phonology, and graphology must all come into play to a greater or lesser degree.

For while stylistic diagnosis or identification can rely upon one or two features selected from the language of texts as being sufficient evidence of stylistic uniqueness, a full and explicit statement of style will require a more complex presentation of interrelated features. It may be sufficient, if evidence of authorship is all that is required, to use a computer to determine quantitatively the density in a given text of one or two specific linguistic features; but this is diagnosis, not description. And the features chosen for this purpose may not, indeed probably will not, be features which are stylistically significant in terms of literary response and artistic effect. Or we may identify the style of a writer by referring simply to his preference for certain words, or his predilection for a particular clause structure; and this would certainly bring us nearer to the heart of the matter. But it seems probable that the secret of individual style can never lie in one dominant feature alone; rather, an explicit statement will need to take account of the inter-relation of many parts which make up the whole. Only by careful descriptive studies can these be brought to the surface and weighed one against the other in terms of our developing responses.

In such descriptive studies it needs to be remembered that any item in the text may be significant in relation to more than one system, or to more than one aspect of form; and the nature of the linguistic features thought to be significant will determine with which system or aspect the detailed descriptive work begins. Nor need any requirement be laid down in advance regarding the degree of delicacy to which any part of the description should be pursued; this must depend upon judgement, as the description proceeds, of the significance or otherwise of a particular feature.

6

A DETAILED analysis of linguistic features within the text has as one of its aims to cut beneath the generalizations, to get behind the metaphorical labels, of which the literary study of style makes such use. It has always been possible, and indeed valuable, to discuss style in literature by reference simply to the general effect upon all aspects of our sensibility of which we are conscious when we dwell upon a work of literary art. Such was the course which Middleton Murry set himself in his Oxford Lectures on *The Problem of Style*[1] forty years ago, and he stands in the mainstream of literary stylistics in so doing. But one is then reduced to the use of terms sufficiently all-inclusive and metaphorical to embrace both the response and the organization of language which is assumed to produce that response. Thus, a 'grand' style presumably offers the reader a sense of grandeur, a 'plain' style a feeling of adequacy without ornament, or a 'baroque' style reminds the reader of a particular kind of architecture. Such shorthand terms are evocative, and fulfil their purpose in so far as they refer to the same response in everyone; and they have therefore considerable use in literary criticism as general categories. They do, however, tend to conflate statements about language with statements about the effects produced by language, and, as Murry recognizes in his opening paragraph,[2] they have a habit, like many critical terms, of sliding out of their accustomed place in the framework of literary description if too carefully scrutinized.

A detailed examination of stylistic effects, as opposed to metaphorical labelling, will inevitably lead us to ask the question: 'If it is said (or if we feel) that this particular style is 'grand', or 'plain', or 'sinewy', in what particular respect does the language provide evidence of grandeur, plainness or sinewy-ness? Are there linguistic correlates to the responses we experience and so label?' Such questions are worth asking, and if the answers provide insufficient clues for the analyst to work upon, it is necessary to return again and again to the response, as it develops, to see whether more specific clues cannot be found and a more precise account of it given.

1. London, 1922.

2. 'It is, I believe, a fairly common experience for those who have been engaged for a good many years in the profession of literary criticism, to slip, almost unconsciously, into a condition of mistrust of all their most familiar and general terms. The critic becomes dissatisfied with the vagueness of his activity, or his art . . .', *op. cit.*, p. 1.

Any linguistic feature may of course possess stylistic significance, but it can be no part of a brief presentation such as this to attempt to list them in detail. To do so would, in fact, produce a catalogue of almost every formal and contextual feature in the language. By way of exemplifying the range, and interrelatedness, of features which may, in different texts, be stylistically significant, therefore, a summary of a few of these will now be made. They have been chosen partly for the illumination they offer of certain stylistic effects and devices often observed but rarely described in detail, and partly also in order to suggest a few lines of inquiry which might bear fruit if pursued in detail in a variety of literary texts.

In the first place, the contribution of grammatical features to stylistic effect has not been much considered or analysed, apart from the generalized, and again often metaphorical, references to the 'rolling' periods or the 'involved' syntax of a writer's language. Concepts of syntactical complexity and simplicity often underly statements of this kind. Linguistic complexity is difficult to measure objectively; but it is possible to describe it in grammatical (and lexical) terms without necessarily quantifying the differences thus exposed. There are, however, not only many degrees of complexity, but many different kinds of complexity; and similarly, a great variety of types of simplicity.

Long sentences do not, of course, necessarily produce a sense of complexity, or what may be termed density of texture. If the clausal relations are paratactic, as they often are in Malory or William Morris, for example, the structure of the prose, being merely additive, is unlikely to give the impression of complexity, other aspects of the text being, so to speak, equal. On the other hand, syntactical hypotaxis is likely to produce the effect of dense, involuted texture, as in much of Henry James' later prose; the rank-shifting which hypotaxis necessarily involves will probably provide, at least in part, a clue to the nature and degree of this complexity. It is clear that the syntactical 'texture' of language may be analysed and tested by grammatical description, provided the grammatical categories and scales which we use enable us to locate different types and degrees of complexity at different places and different 'depths', in terms of the structural patterning which units of differing ranks display.

If, for example, as even a casual reading of many of Sir Thomas Browne's paragraphs suggests, there is carefully contrived syntactical 'balance', it is only by means of a sophisticated grammar that the nature of this balance can be properly discovered and described. In most cases such 'balance', and in Browne even 'palindromic' structure—though he never, it seems, managed a perfect syntactical quincunx in a sentence or paragraph—can be located at one rank, with structural asymmetry at other ranks providing the necessary counterpoise and contrast. Alternatively, balance may be evident at primary structure, but varied by asymmetry at secondary structure. The 'echo' effect of reiteration in dramatic and rhetorical prose is often of this kind, in that it results from syntactical repetition at one rank, with variation at another. This is also characteristic of much poetry and is highly indicative, for example, of the 'set towards the message' in T. S. Eliot's 'Ash Wednesday'.

Syntactical effects in poetry not only include complexity and recurrence, but also syntactical ambiguity. Lexical ambiguity has long been recognized in the metaphor, the pun, and other types of imagery, but it is important to observe that ambiguity is not restricted to lexis. The syntax of poetry probably deserves more attention than it has hitherto received, particularly since verse, however 'free', has a double set of units: those of the line and the stanza, and those of syntax. Often one set is used in counterpoint with the other; in the same way that, at the phonological level, metrical patterns are often counterpointed with the rhythms of speech. It is therefore possible for a poet, by juxtaposing grammatical boundaries with those of the metrical line, to make use of syntactical expectancy, followed by syntactical resolution or surprise. In this way alternative syntactical patterns are able to co-exist, thus contributing to the complexity of the verse.

In the drama and the novel, differentiation between dialogue, monologue, and narrative, or between speakers, is commonly made by grammatical means, though normally with the aid of lexical and graphological features which support and intensify these differences. Interior monologue in James Joyce's *Ulysses*, for example, is usually marked either by syntactical incompleteness or by full syntax without punctuation. Shakespeare and other dramatists often use incomplete or unresolved syntactical patterns, those major characteristics of spontaneous spoken language, to give the impression of a character intellectualizing under strain or in a condition of emotional shock.[1]

A further case which may be instanced where a writer uses grammatical means to produce deliberate effects in his presentation of dialogue is that of Dickens, whose novels richly illuminate the manifold use to which a skilful handling of linguistic differences in speech can be put. An instance of this is his syntactical variation in the presentation of speech in many of his courtroom scenes. A careful examination reveals several different 'degrees' of indirect speech; in some cases it is not possible for the reader to determine whether the author is presenting speech directly, or question and answer conflated, or an indirect summary of the speech of the courtroom, so carefully does Dickens withdraw, partially or wholly, at different points, the grammatical markers of indirect speech.

Syntactical investigations of this kind, if they are intended as a contribution to detailed and explicit statements about style, must of course be matched with, and checked against the results of careful examinations of the lexis and potential phonology of the texts in question. For grammar can only be a partial contributor to most of these effects. The grammar may display complexity of a particular kind; but lexis may also contribute, and phonological patterning may reinforce syntactical or lexical effects. The intricacy with which collocation and set are managed may, even

1. See e.g. Shakespeare, *Works* (ed. P. Alexander), London, 1951: *Winter's Tale*, I, ii, 121–7; *Cymbeline*, III, ii, 1–17; *Richard III*, V, iii, 182–93.

with a comparatively simple syntax, produce similar, though never precisely the same, effects of involved texture and complexity. Dylan Thomas's poem 'Fern Hill' has a fairly simple syntax, far simpler than that of some of his poems; what complexity the poem has is largely the result of an intricate manipulation of sets and collocations within a relatively complicated metrical form.

In the investigation of the style of a text or of an author through the examination of lexis, particularly the lexical aspect of imagery, considerable work of great perception and consequent influence has been accomplished over the past thirty years, ranging from the seminal work of Wolfgang Clemen and Caroline Spurgeon, to the highly personal yet stimulating Shakespearean 'interpretations' of George Wilson Knight.[1] Nor is it possible to underestimate the contribution made to an appreciative handling of the 'words on the page' by William Empson's *Seven Types of Ambiguity* and *The Structure of Complex Words*.[2] In the field of Romance studies, Leo Spitzer's 'etymological' approach,[3] and Stephen Ullmann's lexical, grammatical, and interpretative work on *l'image littéraire*[4] have opened up other ways of approaching this aspect of language in literary use, ways which have perhaps been somewhat neglected by scholars whose concern is English literature. In face of the available scholarship of quality on this aspect of style, we wish only to suggest the likelihood of increased rigour and the possibility of further insights provided by the theory of lexis, and to offer a few further points.

1. See e.g. Wolfgang Clemen, *Shakespeares Bilder, ihre Entwicklung und ihre Funktionen im dramatischen Werk*, Bonn, 1935 (English translation: *The Development of Shakespeare's Imagery*, London, 1951); C. F. E. Spurgeon, *Shakespeare's Imagery*, Cambridge, 1935; G. Wilson Knight, *The Wheel of Fire*, London, 1930, *The Imperial Theme*, London, 1931, *The Shakespearean Tempest*, London, 1932.

2. London, 1930 and 1951 respectively.

3. See e.g. *Linguistics and Literary History*, Princeton, 1948, and *A Method of Interpreting Literature*, Northampton, Mass., 1949.

4. See esp. *Style in the French Novel*, Cambridge, 1957, *The Image in the Modern French Novel*, Cambridge, 1960, and *Language and Style*, Oxford, 1964.

There are, it appears, twin yet opposed perils in 'imagery-conscious' criticism. On the one hand, there is the danger of over-emphasizing the importance of a group of images or, for that matter, a lexical set which is statistically dominant. There may be in Shakespeare a great many images drawn from nature, but is this necessarily of significance in the work of an author of the non-industrial sixteenth century who lived his life in a Warwickshire and London which would seem very rural to us now? On the other hand, there is the danger of a critic's over-emphasizing the significance of an image of little statistical prominence which has greatly interested him, perhaps for highly personal reasons. In this matter, as in others in the analysis of style, a dialectic between the subjective response and the objective description seems likely to develop the most useful critical statement.

As was noted earlier, when examining lexis it is best to be aware that lexical ambiguity may have, as a concomitant, grammatical and phonological ambiguity. In John Donne's 'A Hymn to God the Father', we have the pun through homophony of 'done', the past participle form of the verb 'do', and the noun word 'Donne', the author's name. An examination of the possible syntactical ambiguities resulting from the different word classes of the alternatives, their differing potentiality of operation in structure, suggest that Donne, in this case, perhaps made greater use of the possibilities for ambiguity provided by the grammar and phonology of his time than is realized if notice is taken only of the lexical pun. The rank-shifted clause 'though it were done before' in the first sentence of the poem:

> Wilt thou forgive that sinne where I begunne,
> Which is my sin, though it were done before?

has two possible structures: A(though) S(it) P(were done) A(before), and A(though) S(it) P(were) A(Donne before); 'Donne before' is a reversal of the normal nominal group at adjunct order of binder (before) and head (Donne), but not intolerable in verse. The meaning we reach from relating the grammatical and lexical

form of the second analysis to the situation of the poem is not in-
consistent with, rather it amplifies, the thought of the poem, in
that it focuses on the idea of Original Sin: that which made
necessary the redemptive act of Christ, which is one of the concerns of the final stanza. The sin with which Donne began was
done before, was before Donne.

The penultimate line of the first two stanzas:

> 'When thou hast done, thou hast not done,'

has four possible analyses, all of which contribute, as we try to
indicate in the italicized glosses, to the effect of the poem:

A [r/s clause: A(When)S(thou)P(hast done)] S(thou)P(hast not done)
When you have finished (forgiving), you have not finished

A [r/s clause: A(When)S(thou)P(hast)C(Donne)]S(thou)P(hast not)C(Donne)
When you have John Donne, you have not John Donne

A [r/s clause: A(When)S(thou)P(hast)C(Donne)] S(thou)P(hast not done)
When you have John Donne, you have not finished (forgiving)

A [r/s clause: A(When)S(thou)P(hast done)] S(thou)P(hast not)C(Donne)
When you have finished (forgiving), you have not John Donne

The ambiguity of the penultimate line of the third and final
stanza, 'And, having done that, Thou hast done', is, perhaps
fittingly, less complex: only two analyses are possible because
there are alternative analyses only in the non-rank-shift part of
the clause. The non-finite rank-shift clause at adjunct, 'having
done that' has its complement in 'that', so that 'done' is unambiguously the head of the verbal group at predicator. Thus:

A [non-finite r/s clause: P(having done)C(that)] S(Thou)P(hast done)
                                       and S(Thou)P(hast)C(Donne)
*When you have assured me of the saving grace of your Son at my death, O God, you
have finished and you have John Donne.*

The examination of the way language is used in this poem, a
'concentration on the set towards the message' demands then a
recognition that the graphological exponents 'done' and 'Donne'
represent the same phonological exponent of two distinct lexical
items, and forms of two distinct word classes offering two distinct

structural possibilities. Linguistic description may not only produce such recognition, it can also help to explicate it, and an insistent emphasis on the potential need for all aspects of formal description (grammatical, lexical, phonological, and graphological) as well as contextualization, is therefore by no means out of place in a discussion of stylistic analysis.

7

ASPECTS of contextualization have also been the concern of linguists, and modern linguistic theory offers the concept of *context of situation*. In 1950 the late J. R. Firth wrote:[1]

A key concept in the technique of the London group is the concept of *context of situation*. The phrase "context of situation" was first used widely in England by Malinowski... Malinowski's context of situation is a bit of the social process which can be considered apart and in which a speech event is central and makes all the difference, such as the drill sergeant's welcome utterance on the square "Stand at ease". The context of situation for Malinowski is an ordered series of events considered *in rebus*.

My view was, and still is, that "context of situation" is best used as a suitable schematic construct to apply to language events, and that it is a group of related categories at a different level from grammatical categories, but rather of the same abstract nature. A context of situation for linguistic work brings into relation the following categories:

A. The relevant features of participants: persons, personalities.
    (i) The verbal action of the participants.
    (ii) The non-verbal action of the participants.
B. The relevant objects.
C. The effect of the verbal action.

It is clear that context of situation was thought of by Malinowski and Firth primarily in relation to spoken language, and it has

1. 'Personality and Language in Society', *The Sociological Review*, XIII, 3, 1950, reprinted in J. R. Firth, *Papers in Linguistics*, London, 1957.

indeed been used by linguists mainly in the examination of non-literary linguistic events, and particularly those occurring in the spoken mode. Unfortunately, until recently, too little research and too little discrimination has been applied to this concept in contemporary linguistics and so it remains, as yet, largely un-developed.[1] Suitably modified and extended, however, the concept can be of value both in the understanding of the process of stylistic study and in the process itself. It ensures that any procedures followed in the study of style do not restrict themselves exclusively to an examination of the language of the text.

A literary text may be said to have a context of situation in the sense in which it was understood by Firth. A text may, that is, be regarded as an 'utterance' which is part of a complex social process; and therefore the personal, social, linguistic, literary, and ideological circumstances in which it was written need, as literary scholars have always recognized, to be called upon from time to time when any serious examination of a literary text is being made, be it for the purpose of stylistic or indeed any literary study. Recourse to factors such as these may be termed *cultural contextualization*. Although this is often thought of as becoming, for example, a seventeenth-century man in order to appreciate a seventeenth-century text, the process is rather more complex. It requires the ability to glance from one's own cultural position to that of the contemporary reader, and back again, allowing features in the text to appear in relief by means of a kind of stereoscopic vision. Cultural contextualization is also necessary for a modern text, since cultural positions are, in any absolute sense, unique.

Some of the linguistic aspects of this contextualizing process have already been referred to when we indicated the importance of 'placing' the language of the text in terms of its diachronic (period), diatopic (dialect), and diatypic (field, mode and tenor) status (Section 5), and the necessity for a linguistic to have an historical dimension (Section 4), even if the study is concerned

1. See, however, Notes 1 and 2, p. 68 and Dixon, *op. cit.*, p. 48.

solely with modern texts, because the creative writer lives in a literary and linguistic tradition, and is often significantly conscious of it. Of considerable importance for our purposes, however, is that context of situation which certain literary genres seem especially to allow the writer to create within the text itself. Genre-consciousness, particularly of the dramatic, first-person narrative and monologue types, may be seen as one of those factors which enables the creative writer to draw our attention away from the 'real' context of situation of his work (the addresser-addressee situation and the relevant circumstances of this) and focus it on the 'context of situation' the work itself is creating. Part of the willing suspension of disbelief of being an audience or reader of such works is that we allow the former context of situation to recede into the background, and this created one to come into the foreground, of our attention. This must be taken account of in stylistic study—it is part of our data—even if the latter context is, so to speak, embedded in the text with the result that there can be no clear separation, in its case, of text from situation. There is no formal linguistic way of dealing with this. One must contextualize, summarizing the situation the language is creating. In dealing with any portion of a text this contextualization may for certain descriptive purposes be delimited to a specified segment of it. This may be termed the *immediate intratextual context*. Moreover, the reader of a literary work has increasingly available as he proceeds an accumulation of contextual information against which dialogue, monologue, dramatic action, description of situation and mood, internal allusion, etc., may be placed. This may be called the *accumulated intratextual context*. By the end of the text he is thus in possession of the *total intratextual context*.

In the stylistic examination of a literary work use may well be made of all previously mentioned contextualizations, both extratextual and intratextual. This 'reading with a sense for continuity, for contextual coherence, for wholeness'[1] must be an es-

1. René Wellek, 'Closing Statement from the Viewpoint of Literary Criticism'. Sebeok, *op. cit.*, p. 149.

sential part of stylistic study; it is a necessary check on the equally necessary discreteness which any aspectual work on a text, linguistic or otherwise, requires.

When examining style, and using linguistics in so doing, the analyst should, we believe, not only take into account linguistic features in isolation, but also consider their relation to other aspects of the text and its contextual setting. Otherwise his final statements will be merely linguistic.

8

ANOTHER major difference between a stylistic and a linguistic statement is that the former is necessarily comparative.[1] All concepts of style involve a consciousness of norms and the possibility of departures from them. The comparison may be implicit when an awareness of norms, the product of a developed literary or linguistic intuition, or preferably both, lies behind a comment on the style of a particular text. The stylistically significant linguistic features of a text, however, can often be more clearly observed and more effectively presented when an explicit comparison with another text is made, or used as a 'control' in the process of stylistic examination. Its purpose in the latter case is to help the analyst to view the linguistic features of the central text with a due sense of proportion. Comparative procedures of these kinds reduce, though they do not dispense with, reliance upon impressionistically determined norms. The texts to be used for com-

1. It might however be argued that any linguistic statement about a particular text is necessarily comparative if it is arrived at by 'methods derived by general linguistic theory, using the categories of the description of the language as a whole'. (M. A. K. Halliday, 'The Linguistic Description of Literary Texts', *loc. cit.*). But this is of course comparison of a different nature.

parative and/or control purposes should clearly be neither too similar (unless we are concerned with 'group styles') nor too dissimilar: in the former case only at a hypothetical degree of extreme delicacy would any significantly contrastive linguistic features emerge; in the latter instance the differences would be so gross as to make any detailed analysis merely otiose.

That comparison is an essential part of stylistic study has been recognized by a number of linguists, and they have included it in their definitions of style or stylistics. Enkvist suggests that

The style of a text is a function of the aggregate of the ratios between the frequencies of its phonological, grammatical and lexical items, and the frequencies of the corresponding items in a contextually related norm.[1]

Halliday maintains that

We can define linguistic stylistics as the description of literary texts, by methods derived from general linguistic theory, using the categories of the description of the language as a whole; and the comparison of each text with others, by the same and by different authors in the same and in different genres.[2]

Our concern here is to point out the importance of developed response and intuition in the determination of what is a 'contextually related norm' (the only alternative being intolerably extensive and expensive computer programmes), and to stress the necessity of relevance in the choice of texts for comparison. The present authors would not agree with Halliday's suggestion in the same paper that 'the only relevant exponent of the "might have been" of a work of literature is another work of literature'. The developed literary intuition has always had an idea of the poem the poet might have written.

It is clear that a range of types of comparison may be used, that the style of a text may be examined in relation to:

1. Impressionistically recognized norms of language use;
2. Texts by other authors recognized by reference to 1 as comparable;
3. Other texts by the same author recognized by reference to 1 and 2 as comparable.

1. Present volume, p. 28.
2. 'The Linguistic Description of Literary Texts', *loc. cit.*

By means of all or any of such comparisons both shared and unique features are constantly brought into contrastive relief. For it is worth recalling that since the quality of uniqueness depends upon the prior postulation of shared characteristics, any statement about the style of a text, although it may appear to be made in absolute terms and be concentrated upon unique features alone, is in fact the result of some procedure or other which involves comparative reference.

9

INITIAL readings, 'placing' of the texts, a detailed description of its language, further contextualization (intra- and extra-textual), comparisons made with other texts examined in the same way: these are the main factors in the approach to style suggested here. Among them there is meant to be a constant cross-checking. Personal responses and impressionistically determined norms interact with largely objective linguistic description in the process of stylistic study. This is not intended as a Spitzerian 'circle of understanding' but rather, because responses are open to development and modification as this subjective-objective dialectic proceeds, a 'spiral' appreciation of the use of language in literary texts. In this view the study of the style of a text involves the progressive development and explication of a response which results from a primary, but not an exclusive, concentration on an examination of the complex of linguistic features possessed by that text, both those unique to it and those which it shares with others.[1]

1. Cf. Dell H. Hymes, *op. cit.*, p. 109: 'Style may be investigated both as deviations from a norm and as "a system of coherent ways or patterns of doing things".' In the approach presented here both kinds of investigation are involved, the latter being primary and the former contained within it.

Such a study may be seen as part of what has been called 'literary philology'—'the interpretation of literature in the light of linguistic structure and its history'.[1]

It is not claimed that this is the only tenable view of the study of style. We have simply attempted to assimilate to our own approach what seems most valuable and relevant in the work of both literary critics and linguists,[2] remembering that 'like other high-order abstractions the concept of style has many facets, and can be approached from a variety of angles'.[3] We have tried to sketch in one angle without erasing the others.

1. J. B. Carroll, *The Study of Language*, Harvard, 1955, p. 65.

2. We are very much in accord with Edward Stankiewicz, when he writes: 'the student of poetry is in no position to describe and explain the nature of poetic language unless he takes into account the rules of language which determine its organisation, just as the linguist cannot properly understand the forms of poetic expression unless he considers the forces of tradition and culture that affect the specific character of poetry. The understanding and explication of an original poetic work is, however, always a matter of insight and intuition on the part of the analyst. And since the object of our analysis is broader than our descriptions, which are always of a provisional character, no analysis can be fully exhaustive. Nor can it replace the aesthetic and emotional impact produced by a work of art itself.'—'Linguistics and the Study of Poetic Language', Sebeok, *op. cit.*, p. 81.

3. S. Ullmann, *Style in the French Novel*, p. 1.

Bibliography

WHAT follows is a short, highly selective list of writings in English concerned with style and related fields of study. It is divided into three major sections. Section I consists of books on style and rhetoric written from what might be termed the *literary critical standpoint*; with a few exceptions, works on the style of particular authors have been omitted. Section II consists of two sub-sections, one of books (i) and one of articles (ii), on style from a *linguistic standpoint*. Some items could have been placed in I or II (i), and it is recognized that personal choices have been made in this matter of categorization. A selection of books, and two important articles, on linguistics and related disciplines, which might be of interest to those readers unacquainted with these branches of language study, constitutes Section III; items marked * are thought particularly suitable for initial, introductory reading.

Michael Gregory.

I

Bateson, F. W.—*English Poetry and the English Language.* Oxford, 1934.
Berry, Francis—*Poet's Grammar: person, time and mood in poetry.* London, 1958.
Brooke-Rose, C.—*A Grammar of Metaphor.* London, 1958.
Brooks, C. and Warren, R. P.—*Fundamentals of Good Writing.* London, 1952.
Burke, Kenneth—*The Philosophy of Literary Form.* Louisiana, 1940.
Clemen, W. H.—*The Development of Shakespeare's Imagery.* London, 1951.
Davie, Donald—*Articulate Energy: an enquiry into the syntax of English poetry.* New York, 1958.
Dobrée, Bonamy—*Modern Prose Style.* Oxford, 1934.
Empson, William—*Seven Types of Ambiguity.* London, 1930.
Empson, William—*The Structure of Complex Words.* London, 1951.
Foerster, N.—*Literary Scholarship, its aims and methods.* Chapel Hill, 1941.
Grierson, H. J. C.—*Rhetoric and English Composition.* (2nd ed.), London, 1945.
Lewis, C. Day—*The Poetic Image.* London, 1947.

Lewis, C. S.—*Studies in Words*. Cambridge, 1960.

Lucas, F. L.—*Style*. London, 1955.

Murry, John Middleton—*The Problem of Style*. Oxford, 1922.

Nowottny, W.—*The Language Poets Use*. London, 1962.

Quiller-Couch, Sir Arthur—*The Art of Writing*. Cambridge, 1916.

Raleigh, Sir Walter—*Style*. London, 1897.

Rannie, D. W.—*The Elements of Style*. London, 1915.

Read, Sir Herbert—*English Prose Style*. London, 1928.

Richards, I. A.—*Principles of Literary Criticism*. London, 1924.

Richards, I. A.—*Practical Criticism*. London, 1929.

Richards, I. A.—*The Philosophy of Rhetoric*. New York, 1936.

Ricks, C. B.—*Milton's Grand Style*. Oxford, 1963.

Rylands, G.—*Words and Poetry*. London, 1928.

Spurgeon, C. F. E.—*Shakespeare's Imagery*. Cambridge, 1935.

Strunk, Jr., W., and White, E. B.—*The Elements of Style*. New York, 1959.

Warren, A. and Wellek, R.—*Theory of Literature*. New York, 1949.

Wimsatt, W. K.—*The Prose Style of Samuel Johnson*. New Haven, 1941.

Wimsatt, W. K. and Beardsley, M. C.—*The Verbal Icon*. Kentucky, 1954.

Wimsatt, W. K. and Brooks, C.—*Literary Criticism: a short history*. New York, 1957.

II (i)

Allen, H. B.—*Readings in Applied English Linguistics* (Part 7). New York, 1958.

Hatzfield, H.—*A Critical Bibliography of the New Stylistics*. Chapel Hill, 1952.

Levin, S. R.—*Linguistic Structures in Poetry*. The Hague, 1962.

Quirk, Randolph—*The Use of English*. London, 1962.

Sebeok, T. (ed.)—*Style in Language*. Cambridge, Mass., 1960.

Spitzer, Leo—*Linguistics and Literary History: Essays in Stylistics*. Princeton, 1948.

Spitzer, Leo—*A Method of Interpreting Literature*. Northampton, Mass., 1949.

Ullmann, S.—*Style in the French Novel*. Cambridge, 1957.

Ullmann, S.—*The Image in the French Novel*. Cambridge, 1960.

Ullmann, S.—*Language and Style*. Oxford, 1964.

Warburg, J.—*The Best Chosen English: introduction to a programme of research*. London, 1961.

Whatmough, J.—*Poetic, Scientific and Other Forms of Discourse*. Cambridge, 1956.

Whatmough, J.—*Language: A Modern Synthesis* (Chapter 6). New York, 1956.

Yule, G. U.—*The Statistical Study of Literary Vocabulary*. Cambridge, 1944.

II (ii)

Alonso, Amado—'The Stylistic Interpretation of Literary Texts'—*Modern Language Notes*, LVII, pp. 489–96, 1942.

Barber, C. L.—'Some Measurable Characteristics of Modern Scientific Prose' —*Gothenburg Studies* 14, *English Syntax and Philology*, 1963.

Harris, Zellig S.—'Discourse analysis'—*Language* 28, pp. 1–30, 1952.

Hatzfield, H.—'The Language of the Poet'—*Studies in Philology* XLIII, pp. 93–120, 1946.

Hatzfield, H.—'Stylistic Criticism as Art-minded Philology'—*Yale French Studies*, II, pp. 62–70, 1949.

Hill, A. A.—'Towards a literary analysis'—(English Studies in honour of James Southall Wilson)—*University of Virginia Studies*, 4, pp. 147–165, 1951.

Hill, A. A.—'An Analysis of "The Windhover": an experiment in structural method'—*Publications of the Modern Language Association of America*, 70, pp. 968–78, 1955.

Hill, A. A.—'A program for the definition of literature'—*Univ. of Texas Studies in English*, 37, pp. 46–52, 1958.

Hornstein, L. H.—'Analysis of Imagery: A Critique of Literary Method'— *Publications of the Modern Language Association of America*, 57, pp. 638–53, 1942.

Levy, R.—'A New Credo of Stylistics'—*Symposium*, pp. 321–34, 1949.

McIntosh, A.—'Patterns and Ranges'—*Language*, 37, pp. 325–37, 1961.

McIntosh, A.—'As You Like It: A Grammatical Clue to Character'—*Review of English Literature*, IV, 2, 1963.

McIntosh, A.—'Grammar and Style'—*Durham Univ. Journal*, 1963.

Riffaterre, M.—'Criteria for Style Analysis'—*Word*, XV, pp. 154–74, 1959.

Riffaterre, M.—'Stylistic Context'—*Word*, XV, pp. 154–74, 1959.

Stutterheim, C. F. P.—'Modern Stylistics'—*Lingua*, I, pp. 410–26, 1947–8, and III, pp. 52–63, 1952–3.

Whitehall, H.—'From Linguistics to Criticism'—*Kenyon Review*, XVIII, pp. 411–21, 1956.

Whitehall, H.—'From Linguistics to Poetry'—*English Institute Essays*, pp. 134–45, 1956.

III

Abercrombie, David—*The Elements of General Phonetics*. Edinburgh, forthcoming.

Bloomfield, L.—*Language*. London, 1935.

*Carroll, J. B.—*The Study of Language*. Oxford, 1953.

Catford, J. C.—*A Linguistic Theory of Translation*. Oxford, 1965.

Chomsky, N.—*Syntactic Structures*. The Hague, 1957.

Dixon, R. M. W.—*Linguistic Science and Logic*. The Hague, 1963.

Firth, J. R.—*Papers in Linguistics*. London, 1957.

Gleason, H. A.—*Introduction to Descriptive Linguistics*. New York, 1955.

*Hall, R. A.—*Linguistics and Your Language*. New York, 1960 (2nd edition).

Halliday, M. A. K.—'Categories of the Theory of Grammar'—*Word*, 17, 3, 1961.

Halliday, M. A. K.—'The Tones of English'—*Archivum Linguisticum*, XV, i, 1963.

*Halliday, M. A. K., McIntosh, A., and Strevens, P.—*The Linguistic Sciences and Language Teaching*. London, 1964.

Hill, A. A.—*Introduction to Linguistic Structures*. New York, 1958.

Hockett, C. F.—*A Course in Modern Linguistics*. New York, 1958.

*Jespersen, O.—*Mankind, Nation and Individual from a Linguistic Point of View*. London, 1946.

Nida, E.—*Synopsis of English Syntax*. Norman, Oklahoma, 1960.

*Potter, S.—*Modern Linguistics*. London, 1957.

*Sapir, E.—*Language*. New York, 1921.

*Sapir, E.—*Culture, Language and Personality*. Cambridge, 1960.

Ullmann, S.—*Semantics: An Introduction to the Science of Meaning*. Oxford, 1962.